Praise for *The Audien*

"I wish I'd had this book before starting Wondery. Tom Webster's understanding of the audio industry from every perspective makes everything he writes a must-read."

HERNAN LOPEZ, founder of Wondery

"Two things I know for sure: Tom Webster is always ahead of audio trends, and if you haven't put real time and effort into getting to know your audience, your podcast isn't as good as it could be. In *The Audience Is Listening*, Webster does a masterful job of taking what he's learned in thirty years of podcast audience research and explaining in clear, simple terms how podcasters of any size can use his insights to grow."

DENNIS CLARK, EVP of talent development at iHeartMedia National Programming Group

"Discover how to do your best work inside this Trojan horse of a book. Yes, it's about podcasting. But what Tom Webster has done (that sly dog!) is give you a blueprint to crafting work you're proud of and that your audience will love. Oh—and 'Episode Three: What We Talk about When We Talk about Podcasts' is alone worth the price on the cover."

ANN HANDLEY, *Wall Street Journal*–bestselling author of *Everybody Writes* and CCO at MarketingProfs

"Got an idea for a podcast? Already making one but not sure how to get it out there? This clear, concise guide is a great way to make the most of your efforts."

MANOUSH ZOMORODI, host of NPR's *TED Radio Hour*

"Not only does Tom Webster lay out a proven method to get your podcast up and running successfully, but he inspires you to improve your game and think big. Everything you need to know about launching a successful podcast and doing it right is in this book, and you can use Webster's blueprint to build a show that attracts listeners while giving you a platform to connect with global audiences. It is evident from his content that he is a wealth of knowledge, with a long history of credible experience in this industry. Your future listeners will thank you for taking his advice."

FATIMA ZAIDI, founder and CEO of Quill and CoHost and podcasting lecturer at the University of Toronto

"Tom Webster has worked with the biggest shows in podcasting and understands the craft of building an audience better than anyone. If you want to turn your podcast into a show, this is the book you need."

JORDAN HARBINGER, creator of *The Jordan Harbinger Show*

"Anytime I need information about the future of audio, podcasting, audio business models, and relevant research, I seek out Tom Webster."

JOE PULIZZI, author of *Content Inc.* and founder of The Tilt

"Fantastic! Tom Webster's deep expertise in audience development shines through. Whether you're a beginner or an industry veteran, you'll learn to understand your audience like never before and put that knowledge to good use growing your show."

MIGNON FOGARTY, Grammar Girl and founder of the Quick and Dirty Tips podcast network

"These are the essential instructions for earning a podcast audience. But more so, a wise and powerful curriculum for all manner of community-building. A must-read not just for podcasters, but for all marketers and business owners."

JAY BAER, author of *The Time to Win*, tequila educator, and host of *The Spirit Guides* podcast

"Tom Webster is the smartest, funniest, and most engaging person in podcasting. This book is overflowing with insights, wisdom, and great storytelling that will help podcasters from beginners to seasoned pros. *The Audience Is Listening* is to podcasters what the *The Elements of Style* is to writers."

STEVE PRATT, co-founder of Pacific Content and author of *Earn It*

"Trust me, producing a podcast is easy. The hard part is getting people to not just listen to it, but to care enough to keep coming back (and to tell everyone they know about it). Tom Webster has forgotten more about podcasting than most people know about it. Full stop. *The Audience Is Listening* will turn any podcast from background noise to must-listen magic. There's audio genius on every page, as Webster shifts away from the standard 'how to grow your audience' to 'how to charm your audience.' This book is witty, excellently crafted, and filled with data-backed insights. So if you want your audience to subscribe and not skip . . . *The Audience Is Listening* is your little guide to building a big podcast."

MITCH JOEL, host of *Six Pixels of Separation: The ThinkersOne Podcast* and *Groove: The No Treble Podcast*

"The biggest mystery in podcasting is the audience—who are they, what do they want, and how can you authentically deliver that to them? No one knows how to answer these questions better than Tom Webster. I sure didn't, until I read this book."

"When it comes to podcasting, there are as many opinions as there are experts. But Tom Webster is one of the only true sages of the art and science of this remarkable medium. This is the essential reference for anyone trying to be a professional podcaster."

"Since the dawn of podcasting, the world has wondered who is listening, what they like, where and when they tune in, and why they act like they do. Tom Webster has done more to provide the answers we seek than anyone anywhere. He is an indispensable asset to the world of podcasting who imparts knowledge with wit, candor, and a twinkle in his eye."

A Little Guide to Building a Big Podcast

Tom Webster

● ● **PAGE TWO**

The Audience Is Listening

Cataloguing in publication information is available
from Library and Archives Canada.
ISBN 978-1-77458-527-6 (paperback)
ISBN 978-1-77458-528-3 (ebook)
ISBN 978-1-77458-529-0 (audiobook)

Page Two
pagetwo.com

Edited by Scott Steedman
Copyedited by John Sweet
Cover and interior design by Taysia Louie

audienceislisteningbook.com

To Tamsen:
my co-host, my great love,
my constant beam.

Contents

Pre-roll
How Do I Get
More Listeners?

Introduction

This is a book about podcasting—specifically, how to make a *better* podcast than the one you have now. Yes, I know the subtitle of this book promises a path to growing your audience. If we are going to get there, we have to agree on this small admission: your podcast could be better. I'm not saying it's terrible! I'm not saying it's *not* terrible. I'm just saying it could be better, and if we can agree on that, then this is the book for you.

As I sit down to write this book, I've been in podcasting for nearly two decades. Yes, I have been a podcaster myself, and I've had shows with millions of downloads, shows with hundreds of downloads, and everything in between. That alone doesn't give me the credibility to write this book. But over that period of time I have served as the principal chronicler of this space from an audience perspective. I attended my first podcasting conference back in 2005, with the goal of understanding exactly what podcasting was so that I could add it to the research efforts of the company I was with at the time, Edison Research, best known in the audio world for its annual Infinite Dial survey, which I worked on for eighteen years.

I took that understanding and added it to the Infinite Dial study for 2006, and it's been a part of that work ever since, measuring and validating the podcast space so that creators could get paid, advertisers could find security, and businesses could be started. In the years since, I have authored or contributed to a large percentage of the most important studies in this space. It has *literally* been my job to understand the podcast audience, and if you google my name and "podcasting," you will see the evidence of my commitment to this space over the years.

What you will not see is all the private work I have done for media organizations over those years to understand *their* audiences, and help them grow their shows and podcasts to their full potential. This is the work that doesn't get shared because it is a part of the competitive advantage for these organizations. Indeed, the only way to maintain a competitive advantage in the media and entertainment business is to continue knowing more about your audience than the competition does.

In all this public and private work in podcasting, I've helped hundreds and hundreds of radio stations, network programs, and podcast companies grow their audiences. When I talk about this work to creators, they are quick to tell me that they don't have the resources of a big company and couldn't possibly do the kind of work to compete at that level. That has bothered me for years. This book is my attempt to bring the same kind of process I have employed with the biggest networks to the individual podcaster, because you have the ability to understand your audience better than anyone. This is your competitive advantage, and I want to help you claim it.

This is *not* a book about how to make a podcast. I am going to assume you know this, at least at some level. Anyway, the tech in podcasting changes all the time. I have little interest in writing a book for you that will be obsolete in a year. No, I promise you that this book will be useful to you *for the rest of your career in podcasting*. Scout's honor.

This is going to be a book of tough love, hard work, and, most importantly, a repeatable process that any podcaster can employ, with little or no money, to put their podcast in a better position to earn and keep an audience. More than anything else, I want this for you. My entire job right now, as a partner in the podcast advocacy and insights firm Sounds Profitable, is to grow the entire space, help people build careers in spoken word audio, and establish podcasting as the major entertainment medium that I (and you) know it rightfully deserves to be. Your job is simply to retain an open mind and come with me.

Deal? Excellent. Let's get started.

How to Lose a Few Pounds

Our journey begins with a trip to London and a seemingly irrelevant question:

Have you ever tried to lose weight?

I sure have. I've had varying degrees of success, but none more successful than a stretch of my life nearly twenty-five years ago where I literally lost *millions* of pounds.

At the end of the twentieth century (wow, does that sound ancient!), I was a successful young executive with the largest pure-play radio company in the world at the time (AMFM—pour one out for my homies), charged with researching the tastes of music and talk radio listeners all over the world. I didn't start out in media research; at one point I was pursuing a career in academia, and even taught Rhetoric and Composition at Penn State for a couple of years as a grad student. Ultimately, my passion for spoken word audio and my natural curiosity for what makes people tick led to a peculiar career in audience research that I doubt my high school guidance counselor could have predicted.

In 1999, though, I was ready for a change. I left a promising career in radio research to move to London and partner with a couple of my former clients in something brand-new (at the time): an internet radio service. To you, reading this now, the concept of "internet radio" must seem quaint. Back then, however, the options were slim. The services at that time consisted of Spinner, NetRadio, AOL Radio, and other names now lost to obscurity. The idea we had was simple: we would offer dozens of stations suited to various genres of music, design some kind of interface to sort people into the stations they would most enjoy, and produce those stations to radio standards, not to internet radio standards.

Fortunately for us, another company also believed in the idea, and funded us to the tune of a couple of million pounds. (You can see where this is going now.) The product we built, Puremix, was *glorious*. We had all the trappings of a hip dot-bomb: flashy office in Clerkenwell, quirkily named conference rooms, foosball table, and the occasional pop star dropping by to do live interviews with our staff of music journalists.

For my part, I conducted the largest survey of music taste in UK history and, working with our music team, designed thirty-six individual radio stations that sounded *fantastic*. Now, thirty-six might not sound like a lot to you, but consider that we were offering four distinct flavors of classic rock to a country that only had one in any given market.

We also aimed to be much more than a music service—we wanted to be a complete music-based entertainment portal. So we hired music journalists from the BBC and elsewhere to source and write entertainment stories, update a concert calendar, and assign all that content based on the music preferences of the user. And I was managing a team of developers with index cards, poster putty, and a large brick wall to code a behemoth content management system to host and sort it all. We were all in over our heads, all working insane hours—but we loved it, and we loved what we built.

On Halloween 1999, we launched Puremix in the UK with a bang. It sounded glorious—like nothing anyone had heard before. To this day, I still don't think it's been equaled, to be honest. Each station sounded alive, with engaging personalities, expertly crafted playlists, promotions, and just a handful of sponsorship messages (not enough, sadly). I loved Puremix. It remains the coolest thing I've ever done, and the fact that it is today so far in my rearview mirror underlines the sadness I feel when I discuss it in those terms. To this day, if you get me talking about Puremix, I will tear up.

It didn't work.

We told ourselves a lot of things at the time, mostly along the lines of "we were just too far ahead of our time." This is no longer a thing I believe. We were most certainly *of* our time, not ahead of it. We knew plenty about the music tastes of our audience, and if they could have listened to our stations, I know they would have loved them. But we did not know enough about how many of them had broadband at home (not many in 1999) or planned to buy it, or how many could listen to music on their work internet (not enough), or how satisfied they were with their existing choices (which were surprisingly good). We knew a lot about our product, but we did not know enough about the humans.

By May 2000, Puremix was shuttered, and everyone given a severance package. I returned to the US and spent the entire summer watching Durham Bulls baseball before deciding to return to graduate school, get an MBA in consumer behavior, and get back on the horse. I had learned a valuable thing: it doesn't matter how passionate you are about audio, or video, or whatever content area you specialize in. *If you don't understand the human at the other end of the screen or speaker, you will never succeed.* This is what I want to teach you without your having to lose a couple of million pounds.

The Most Asked Question in Podcasting

This brings us to you. Or, at least, to who I think and hope you are.

You are a podcaster. You either have or have had a podcast.

I've met literally thousands of you. Not all at once. I'm no Ira Glass. But met you I have—at conferences, events, live shows, in boardrooms. And everywhere I go, nearly every podcaster I meet asks me some variant of the same question:

"How do I get more listeners?"

If the podcaster were a beast on a David Attenborough nature documentary, that would be its plaintive cry.

There is a lot of advice out there about how to be a better podcaster. Much of it is really good. There are wonderful resources available on which mic to use, how to get interviews, the best editing software, and how to use social media to promote your podcast. This book contains almost none of these things. It's not that I don't think they are important—they are. Use the best mic you can afford. It doesn't matter what kind. But audio quality matters. Don't skimp on it. That's all I have to say about microphones. Bad audio quality can undoubtedly lose you a listener. But spending several thousand dollars on a Neumann u85 will *never* satisfy the plaintive cry of the podcaster: "How do I get more listeners?"

Here is the truth about podcasting, and it's time you were told it true. There are two things you can master on your journey to the next level of podcasting: knowledge of your *craft* (audio editing, software, marketing, etc.)

and knowledge of your *audience*. And the harsh reality, my friends, is that nearly every podcaster I talk to spends all their time in column A and none at all in column B. They've been told that they just need to be passionate about their topic and have something to say. I hope that's true for you, of course. But those things are table stakes. They don't guarantee you an audience. *No one* is guaranteed an audience, and no one deserves one, no matter how passionate they are about their topic.

Now, you may not be entitled to an audience, but that doesn't mean you can't earn one. To do that, you need to spend as much time mastering that half of the craft as you do on the technical aspects of podcasting. And like the technology that powers our medium, the audience is also always changing and evolving over time. Like the Red Queen in *Through the Looking-Glass*, we podcasters often have to keep running with the audience just to stay in one place.

This book is about that race. It saddens me whenever I hear people ask other podcasters the existential question of this book ("How do I get more listeners?") and the response they are met with is something like "Facebook ads" or "cross-promotion." Those do not get you an audience. They get you more eyeballs or perhaps even top-of-mind name recognition. They might even get someone to try your podcast, which seems like a good intermediate step. But none of those things create an *audience*—a body of humans who look forward to your show, week after week, and make it a regular part of their lives.

Ultimately, every podcaster is producing an entertainment, a diversion for someone else's time in a universe full of such diversions. In such a universe, the listener is not a commodity to be collected—the listener is in complete control. The audience has always been in control. It is a fickle beast, but not an inscrutable one. You only need to spend some time with them, learning from them, and their secrets become a little less mysterious. It is this arcane knowledge that can turn your *podcast*, an audio enclosure delivered by RSS syndication, into a *show*, a thing people care about enough to tell somebody else about it.

It's that last bit that really matters. Today, with our attention so fragmented across myriad streaming audio and video options, we rely more and more on the recommendations of friends and family for nearly everything we intentionally consume. Indeed, whenever you see research on how people learn about new podcasts, recommendations are at the very top of the list—not TikTok, not Twitter (now X), and not Google. In fact, learning about shows on things like X/Twitter is well down the list; yet most of the marketing advice podcasters are offered revolves around social promotion—because it's *easy*. Easy doesn't mean effective. In truth, many of the podcasts people learn about on social media are from people who are already famous, or at least influencers in their sphere. In other words, people who already *have* an audience. Doesn't seem so easy now, does it?

We get this advice because, ultimately, there are no easy levers to pull to earn word of mouth for your podcast. There is no way for you to increase your "friends and family" marketing budget. The only path to getting more recommendations is to be recommendable. And the only path to "recommendability" is to know as much as possible about what the recommenders—your potential audience—are looking for, lacking, loving, and hating. And this, my friends, involves doing some decidedly unglamorous work: learning as much about your audience as you do about plug-ins and microphones.

I can guarantee you that any podcast near the top of the Apple or Spotify charts knows more about its audience than probably any podcaster reading this knows about theirs. I know because I have done some of that work for them. For the last thirty years, I have been working in audience development for media properties all over the world in radio, TV, content marketing, and, yes, podcasting. I've worked with and even helped to launch some of the most listened-to radio stations in the world, and studied the audiences of shows ranging from Howard Stern and Elvis Duran to *All Things Considered* and everything in between. And for the last nineteen years (nearly as long as podcasting has been around!), I've had the privilege to work with most of the leading producers of podcasts— names like SiriusXM, Wondery, and NPR—to help them understand and better serve their audiences.

As I talk to people who work at various levels in podcasting, I have become more and more aware that this bizarro arcane knowledge I have accumulated over the years about audiences isn't really taught anywhere. I wouldn't know where to get it if I needed it, right now. That, ultimately, is why I decided to write this book: all this weird stuff I have learned about audiences over the years might be able to help podcasters, and if I don't write it down now, it might be lost to the ages when I finally retire to my yacht or hovercraft or wherever I choose to spend my golden years.

So here it is: everything I know about growing a *listener*, not a download. The central question of this entire book—your question—is "How do I get more listeners?" For many, this problem is interpreted as an awareness or discovery issue. A marketing challenge. But those are trailing variables. The problem isn't how to make more people want your podcast.

The problem is how to make a podcast more people want.

The process I am going to outline for you in this book, a system I call the Cycle of Insight, is going to help you fill the promise of your podcast by helping you understand your audience almost as well as you understand your family members. At least, your immediate family. I mean, there's a lot of stuff you don't know about your uncles.

But it's going to do more than that—it's going to give you answers to some of your other questions. During the process of working out why potential listeners do or do not listen to your show, you are going to understand a lot more about who they are, how they want to be communicated with (and not just through your podcast), and even what your show should be about week to week, month to month.

If you do the work. And it isn't easy work. But doing it provides you with a way to think about your show that will have you never again wondering how to find listeners or even what topics your show should cover. In short (and I know I am making some big promises here), what I am going to teach you is an *idea engine*—an infinitely repeatable, endlessly sustainable workflow to build deeper relationships with your listeners that will have them telling their friends about your podcast. I'm also going to make sure that no matter what means you use to promote your show to the wide world (and we will cover some in this book), when the world gets to your store, your shelves will be clean, your merchandise will be compelling, and your podcast will be a show.

So, here we go. Press Play, don't increase the speed to 1.5x, and take good notes. You are about to level up your podcast and grow some listeners.

Episode One
Earning Attention

The Podcast You Want to Make

We are going to spend much of this book taking apart your existing podcast and thoroughly dismantling it to the atomic level before building it back into a lean, mean, audience-building machine. But before we can do that, we have to grapple with a very hard truth, while you decide if this is indeed what you want to do. Ninety-nine times out of a hundred, if you ask a podcaster for tips on how to grow your audience, they will give you marketing, promotional, or advertising advice. This will help you get your podcast in front of an audience. It will not help you keep them.

I've spent nearly two decades talking to podcast creators of all sizes, from the smallest independents to the networks and shows at the very top of the industry's several rankers. While the scale of their efforts vary, they often share a single limiting belief that holds back their potential. It can be summed up by a seemingly positive statement: *You are making the podcast you want to make.*

Now, there is nothing wrong with saying that—I would look like a jerk trying to talk someone out of making the show they want to make. After all, this is why many of us got into podcasting or, indeed, any creative endeavor. You want to make your art. I want you to make your art. Again, to insist otherwise isn't exactly a populist argument.

But.

I can tell you this after a career of talking to tens of thousands of listeners: you do not deserve an audience. You have the right to make your art and the right to make it as you see fit. But no one, from the Hoff-less reboot of *Knight Rider* to Chris Gaines, deserves an audience. That doesn't mean you have to compromise your art. But if you want to earn an audience, you can no longer make the podcast you want to make. *You have to make the podcast they want to hear.*

I think a lot of podcasters intend to do this. They at least have an audience in mind, and they try to make a podcast that contains elements that audience would find interesting or appealing. But "intend" is a pretty weak verb, as far as verbs go. It gives you a general direction, but intentions aren't choices, and ultimately creativity is fueled by decisions, not intentions. I happen to love the word "decide." It's from the Latin *de cadere*, which translates to "cut off." The act of deciding isn't just about choosing what to do. It's also about cutting off that which doesn't achieve the specific goal.

For a podcaster, that means truly understanding your audience and who they are at home, and crafting content that not only speaks to their lives but also removes that which does not. That doesn't mean changing your topic, or your perspective, or your point of view on your subject matter—that is the podcast you want to make. But it does mean changing how you present that message and killing off everything that isn't that.

In practice, this means killing some darlings. This means cutting some tangents, not having certain guests, and even eliminating some favorite stories, if they aren't contributing to how your audience receives your message. This is, in fact, a big part of the process when I put together a keynote speech or a crucial presentation—I have to ruthlessly eliminate some of my favorite stories or spiciest anecdotes when they do not serve the audience I am trying to *earn* at that moment. I put them under the bed and chuckle about them later, but they are part of the talk I want to give, not the talk my audience wants to hear. In pursuing this discipline, I am earning an audience and still achieving my ultimate goals.

I have a friend named Andrew Davis, who is a very successful public speaker. One of the things he talks about in his book with Michael Port (another very accomplished speaker), *The Referrable Speaker*, is his approach to getting keynotes all over the world in a wide variety of industry conferences. Andrew picks a vertical (like "travel" or "municipal government") and immerses himself in every nuance of that industry for a year—he talks to the professionals, learns about their problems, and tries to put himself into their shoes as best he can. After he does this, he devotes himself to booking talks in just that industry. That's not to say that he would say no if the phone rang with an unrelated inquiry; it's just that he is choosing to commit every aspect of his paid speaking outreach to that one vertical. Now, here's the thing: his topic (the speech he wants to give) is generally the same! But he does the work to cut out everything that doesn't matter to the audience he is trying to earn, and that changes how he does it, every time. And when he has achieved his goals in that industry, he switches industries and does it all over again.

It's a lot of work, but if you do that work, that kind of immersion with the audience you hope to earn, you don't have to make the false choice between the podcast you want to make and the one your audience wants to hear. You can have both.

It's too much work, you might say. Sure—only the best podcasts do it.

Recommendability

Still, I think a lot of podcasters believe that there is still "low-hanging fruit" out there—some magical tweet or website where audiences are just waiting to devour their podcast, and that this is somehow easier or more attainable than doing the work to craft a better podcast. But here is what I have learned from talking to hundreds and hundreds of podcasters. When they ask me, "How do I grow my audience?" they are not asking the right question—at least not yet. Invariably, the podcasters who ask me that also tell me that their podcast has plateaued, or hasn't grown in months. Behind the "How do I grow my podcast?" question is an assumption that the problem is just finding more people to get in front of. But if your podcast has plateaued, the question you *should* be asking is: Why did my podcast *stop* growing?

I am going to give you the hard truth here: a podcast stops growing because people stop recommending it. Unless you are in the top 0.001 percent of shows and have a marketing budget that includes paid advertising and promotions at a large scale, the best way for you to grow a sustainable audience is for your show to be good enough to be recommended to others.

In study after study (including many that I authored or worked on), when people are asked how they discover new podcasts, the number one answer is recommendations from friends and family. You can buy ads on podcast apps or Facebook, spend on Google search placement, cross-promote with other shows, even put up billboards—but none of these address the top method of discovery for podcasts. After all, you can't exactly increase your "friends and family" budget, at least not in most countries.

People can recommend you in numerous ways. They can share an episode or clip on social media to their friends. They can talk about your show at work. They can even force their spouse or partner to listen to it by playing it loudly while doing household chores, and I would like to apologize to my wife for that. But you can't *force* that interaction. No amount of search engine manipulation or social media promotion can make people talk about your show. The only way to get people to recommend your show is to have a recommendable show. In other words, a show that people want to talk about, proselytize for, and evangelize to the world.

Increasing the recommendability of your show involves three steps, and you can't skimp on any of them. Here they are in inverse order of importance:

1 **Make your show easy to share**

This means doing away with the NASCAR-like pastiche of logos for podcast apps and vague directions like "check us out wherever you get your podcasts," and giving potential new listeners a single, easy-to-type website for your show that has a big Play button right at the top. Why complicate things? Below that, you can list all the apps and platforms people can use to listen further so that they can pick and choose to their heart's content. Podcasting has already attracted most of the podcast-savvy people it is going to get.

If you truly want to maximize the audience for a podcast called *Potato Chip Reviews*, you need a website at www.potatochipreviews.com with an annoyingly obvious Play button. That doesn't mean you don't then list all the badges and buttons to hear the show elsewhere. But why confuse people from the get-go? Give them one obvious port of entry.

2 **Make your show easy to talk about**

This is going to be the subject of Episode Nine in this book—crafting an economical pitch statement about your show that says exactly who it is for and what those people stand to gain from listening. If we truly want people to evangelize our show, we can't leave the details up to them.

Most people are fairly inarticulate when it comes to positive things. If you ask a Yelp reviewer to say what they liked about a restaurant, they are likely to point to generic things like "the service was good." Ask them for negative feedback, however, and they get detail-oriented real quick, pointing out EXACTLY how the server screwed up their gluten-free selection and didn't bring water until I asked and the rib eye was clearly overdone and there was a crying baby why are there babies allowed in this restaurant it was our anniversary and the night didn't feel very special also they didn't offer us coffee at the end and it was hard to park and it was raining. The bread was good, though.

When most people talk about podcasts positively, they articulate things like "It is funny," or "It's really interesting," or maybe even "It's about a murder." You couldn't even tell the genre of the show from that. We need to give our listeners specific language—who the show is for and why it's perfect for them—so that they can use that language and carry forth our message to the outside world. Again, we will get to that later in the book, because the most important thing we need to do—the subject of the next seven episodes—is this:

3 Make a show worth talking about

When people talk about podcasts on social media, they will use phrases like "It's about the content" or "Content is king." *Make better content* seems like pretty easy advice to agree with, but that advice is rarely followed up with details on how to accomplish that. Fret no more, friends, because I am going to teach you just that. And everything I learned about how to create content that people talk about, I learned from the Song of the Summer.

The Song of the Summer

If you look at the history of streaming TV, the growth of any one platform has never been tied to the technology, or even knowledge that streaming TV exists; it has always been tied to a small number of original shows. *Orange Is the New Black* and *House of Cards* spurred Netflix subscriptions. *The Handmaid's Tale* played a role in growing Hulu. *Star Trek* drove a lot of Paramount+ users. This phenomenon is also true in audio—you needn't look any further than the role Howard Stern plays in SiriusXM satellite radio sign-ups and retention.

Podcasting as a medium had this moment with *Serial*, which became our first water-cooler podcast. But let's be honest here—that was almost ten years ago. Now, I am not one of those who decry podcasting's supposed inability to "create hits," but I do think it is fair to say that the medium has had a shortage of talk-about moments like the kind *Serial* spawned. Can you pin that on content? Partially, but not as much as you might think.

There are loads of great podcasts. We will make loads more. But there are also lessons here in the way podcasts are promoted and in how we talk about them. When we were all watching *Tiger King* at the start of the pandemic, we weren't asking each other, "Hey! Have you tried streaming TV? It's GREAT." No, we all talked about *Tiger King* for a short period of time. *Tiger King* was the Song of the Summer, and we didn't care where it was or what kind of technology carried it. We just wanted to watch it.

The Song of the Summer was something I learned from Frankie Blue, the original program director for WKTU-FM in New York. When the station launched in the '90s (I did all the music research), it was an enormous success—young and old listeners alike tuned in to live or relive their youth with "The Beat of New York." I remember in one music meeting, as I was working with the team on sorting through the latest research and categorizing songs, Frankie said something very wise: "Winning in New York isn't only about consistently playing good music. It is also about winning 'the Song of the Summer.'" That year, it was "Macarena" (I KNOW, I KNOW).

Serial was podcasting's Song of the Summer a long time ago—the song that was emblematic of an entire medium. But consider that *Serial* was not one of dozens or hundreds of podcasts carried by its home network. It was a singular brand extension from a well-established, singular show, *This American Life*. *Serial* was the recipient not just of cross-promotion but of the undivided attention of *TAL*'s promotional focus outside the parent show. Today we get shows dropped every week and promoted for short periods of time or with other podcasts, but *Serial* didn't really have to share the stage, and I am convinced that played a big role in it becoming the Song of the Summer for podcasting.

I recently gave some advice to a friend of mine who has put together a network of multiple podcasts covering a particular subject area; he was running into the same problem all of you have encountered: it's hard to build an audience. My advice to him was to stop promoting all his shows at once and instead to devote his promotional and cross-promotional efforts to the single "flagship" show and let that show, in turn, promote the network. It's just hard to get people to try one thing when we are constantly asking them to try all the things.

That's also why, when I am asked by people who are not regular podcast listeners, I typically recommend a handful of the absolute biggest and best shows. If I am asked by a typical podcast listener what other storytelling podcasts I would recommend, I'll offer a list. But for a newbie? I'm recommending *The Moth*. Fan of investigative journalism? I'm only offering *In the Dark*. And so on. Every new listener to podcasting judges the medium based on their first taste, and we can't afford not to put our best foot forward every time.

I would sum all this up by saying that we aren't quite there yet as far as making podcasting a habit for mainstream consumers. We need more Songs of the Summer, and that requires large segments of listeners to all be talking about the same thing at the same time. And this brings me to the titular problem of this section: podcasting has had some of those moments post-*Serial*, and sadly, they are often about Joe Rogan, which is not the best we have to offer (and not even a podcast now, as far as that goes).

But there he is—by light-years the most popular podcast in America; number two is not even close. Talk to people about trying a podcast and see how many respond with "Oh, like Joe Rogan?" Joe Rogan has put podcasting on the map, in his own way, with regular emissions of effluvia that include anti-science, racism, and junk conspiracy theories. I am not saying Rogan is a bad person. Never met the man. But as the "face" of podcasting for so many humans who have few other interactions with the medium, he is a terrible ambassador for podcasting.

Well, there isn't much I can do about that one. But there is a lesson here for both networks and individuals alike. For publishers, it may be that promotionally you need to focus on one thing at a time for a while, instead of all the things. The music industry has known this for a long time.

And for those of us who talk to friends and family about trying podcasting, all I can do is to remind you all of the Song of the Summer. That there are hundreds of shows about that one weird hobby your father-in-law has may be something he can come to appreciate in time; the variety of podcasting is what keeps us regulars engaged. But variety is only a benefit for those who know and like the choices. If your job is to sell someone new to the medium, have a look at the top shows in podcasting and see if you can't recommend just one of those, at least to start with.

As Head & Shoulders told us in its TV ads for years, you never get a second chance to make a first impression.

Making a Podcast People Hate

Now, I want to put my audience development hat on here and talk about what Joe Rogan does right that so few in podcasting really get: super-serving a core audience.

Rogan's core is exactly who you think they are—young men who spend a lot of time on YouTube and followed Rogan to Spotify. They do listen to other podcasts, as it turns out, but Rogan is certainly a standard-bearer for many of them. You probably have a very clear picture in your head who a Rogan fan is when they are at home— what they look like, listen to, read, and believe. You have this because Rogan is crystal clear about attracting a very specific audience, even at the exclusion of others.

It is this simple fact of marketing that makes me wince anytime I hear someone tell me their podcast is for "everyone" or "anyone with an interest in [topic]." A topic of interest is not an organizational principle—it isn't specific enough. Imagine you were doing a podcast about My Little Pony toys and collecting. There are three distinct groups (at least) who would be interested in this: nine-year-old girls, sixty-year-old dudes with collectible shops, and bronies. I guarantee you cannot make a podcast that appeals to all three of these segments (and the bronies care most about the brand).

That's why *My Favorite Murder* is so good—it's a topic (true crime) with a specific point of view: Karen and Georgia's comedic take on, well, murder. Not everyone is going to like it. But if you like it, you really like it. The famous hotelier Ian Schrager calls it "one plus one equals three." You build something most people will hate but a few people love—and love enough to tell their friends about. For a podcast, that means having as clear a picture about your topic area, point of view, and ideal listener (yes, listener—singular) as you possibly can, and making the podcast that human would love even if most people would hate it.

As long as Rogan is speaking to that one listener, and producing content that polarizes people into camps of "love" and "hate," he's going to print money. The worst thing you can say about a podcast isn't that people hate it, it's that nobody loves it. And make no mistake—Rogan's audience *loves* him, and they love him because he gets exactly who they are.

For those who aren't fans, Rogan's audience might seem like a group of maladjusted stoners who like UFC. Part of doing the work of audience research, though, is to frame every audience positively. When I see Rogan's audience, I see a group of disenfranchised, young (mostly) men who do not feel completely in control of the narrative of their own lives and cannot shake the feeling that the system is rigged against them, because older guys like me continue to hang on to our jobs and aren't sharing the American dream with them. They distrust authority because authority hasn't helped them. And they don't like having information kept from them by gatekeepers of any kind, because gatekeepers (they believe) are also keeping them from doing better. Rogan exposes them to the information they believe society keeps hidden so that they can make their own decisions. They don't want conspiracy for the sake of conspiracy—they want a sense of agency in their own lives.

See? It's not that hard to do, if you cultivate a little empathy. And Joe Rogan super-serves that audience, even to the exclusion of others. And that is the hard part—sometimes you have to lose an existing audience to make these kinds of creative choices. That's tough to take, especially when downloads go down and unhappy emails roll in. It requires some bravery, a strong stomach, and, most importantly, the knowledge that there is a "there" there with the audience segment you are ultimately trying to attract.

I think we are all capable of this; it just requires clarity and hard choices. But we need more Rogans. We need more podcasts that spark passion, with clear points of view, that plant flags for people to rally around. Maybe this is the hardest question to ask yourself as a podcaster: Would anyone rally around this flag?

There are absolutely podcasts out there that I rally around, support financially, and belong to Discord communities for, and I hate Discord. I feel as though I am their only listener—the show was made for me. And if podcasting is going to grow beyond the obvious smash hits, creators have to make a show that truly *earns the attention* of one listener before you can even think about growing an audience.

The Secret to Earning Attention

Capturing attention is just the tip of the iceberg. To maintain that attention requires consistency, discipline, and an unending commitment to audience value. The content needs to start from a familiar ground (my former mentor, Frank Cody, used to say we must challenge the audience but not defeat them) and then introduce novel, surprising, and delightful elements.

Attention is not a goal. Attention is a trailing variable, the result of doing something *truly outstanding*. Either people specifically seek it out or it's so remarkable that it reverberates through word of mouth. The key? It has to be exceptional, like a beacon amidst a sea of mediocrity.

To me, making a podcast that is remarkable requires one or more of these elements:

- It should challenge.
- It should come from genuine expertise.
- It should be entertaining.

Achieving one of these is table stakes. Two, and your podcast might be worthy of an audience. All three? You just might be on the way to making something you can be proud of and that genuinely earns attention.

Turning the podcast you want to make into the podcast they want to hear involves knowing what they want to hear! Unfortunately, people aren't always able to tell you that so easily—and they especially aren't particularly good at giving you feedback on new or unfamiliar content, or hypothetical questions about what your show *could* do. That's not because they aren't smart—they just don't think about these things every day. Luckily, there are better ways to get at this information, and there is no better place to start than the most important thing you can know about your audience, which is where we are headed next!

Episode Two
The Most Important Thing to Know about Your Podcast

Don't Ask Me Why

I can tell you this from all my years speaking to audiences: there is no more powerful thing to know about your listeners than why they do, or do not, listen to your show. It's the grail truth. And it's generally one simple thing about your show. Your challenge is to figure out what that thing is, which is not a straightforward task!

You spend a lot more time thinking about the nuances of your podcast than your audience does, which means their ability to talk about exactly why they find your show compelling is naturally going to be limited. Sure, they can say what they like—whether it is a certain segment, or that the host is "funny," or the content is interesting. But there is always a deeper truth to uncover. Why is it interesting? Why are they funny? These are the undercurrents of your show and the key to understanding what really works or doesn't work about your podcast. After all, there are thousands of podcasts on your topic—so why yours?

By the way, this has nothing to do with the popular phrase "know your why." This concept, popularized by Simon Sinek's TEDX Talk, was originally about leadership, not marketing. It suggested that leaders could inspire their teams more effectively if they could get them to buy into the company's overarching "why." However, marketers quickly adopted this idea and applied it to everything from making shoes to building cars.

Here's the thing: We aren't making a backpack. We are crafting an entertainment. No one cares about the "why" behind *Young Sheldon*, or *NCIS*, or *Law and Order*, or *The Voice*. They are all the same, anyway: "We would like to make a profit."

In fact, why YOU are making a podcast is pretty irrelevant to the work of earning an audience. Ultimately, when you launch your podcast out into the world, the reason why you made the thing is less important than the reason why an audience would listen to the thing, and those are not always the same. A podcast, like any other product or service, is a brand—the co-created collision of what you intended it to be and what it was perceived to be. It occupies a position in the mind of the listener: "I listen to this particular show because . . . "

So, in the process of building a better podcast, we do start with the question of why—but there are two twists:

- The most important thing we can know is why people do or do not listen to your podcast.

- There is no single "why."

Their why vs. your why

This is not a book on branding, so I don't want to spend too much time on this topic—it's a book unto itself. But imagine that the reason why you are making your podcast is one circle of the venerable Venn diagram—you know the one, with the two intersecting circles. You probably have goals for your podcast: passive income, thought leadership, part of your sales funnel for other goods and services you offer, or maybe just a creative outlet. Whatever the case, I know you have ambitions, at least, or you wouldn't have bought this book.

Whatever flashed into your head when you read that last paragraph is not why your listeners choose to spend time with your show. They have their own reasons, independent of yours, for listening—that's the other circle. When those differing reasons are congruent—when the two circles overlap—then you have a show that is in alignment with your goals and the goals of your listeners. And when you don't, you don't.

Let me give you two non-podcast examples, since these are a bit more obvious. When Taco Bell was purchased by Pepsi back in the late 1970s, the brand was launched nationwide with a singular why: FRESH. Every Taco Bell ad featured knives cutting through glistening heads of lettuce to seal in the reason for Taco Bell's existence in the first place—a fresh take on fast food. That was the company's why: fresh.

But this was not the customers' why.

No, if you asked loyal Taco Bell customers why they chose the brand over their other fast-food options, you would likely get some combination of "It's late," "I'm broke," and "I'm stoned/drunk." Fresh does not factor into the equation here.

Taco Bell, to its credit, leaned into this perception—it's better that the customer thinks something about you than thinks nothing about you—and today, look at Taco Bell's messaging: open late, food to "Live Mas," and, of course, entire meals made out of Doritos. Taco Bell is a coherent, strong brand because it figured out the why of its customers and simply became that thing over time. (By the way, the original owner of Taco Bell was . . . Glen Bell. Imagine if he were named Glen Wilson or Bloomstein or St. John-Smythe.)

In contrast, GM's defunct Oldsmobile brand is a great example of a product that had a terrible why, hence the defunct part. For GM, the why was to have a high-end brand to slot in between Buick and Cadillac, comfortable but not too ostentatious, and not as performance focused as Cadillac. Its reason for existence was purely for product portfolio management, to ensure there were no gaps in the line. So, what did drivers think about why Olds existed? It was a car for old people. These circles, my friends, were pretty far apart at the end, and that's why I am not driving a Cutlass Supreme to this day. Well, that and they were pretty ugly towards the end. I mean, the Silhouette is an all-timer.

So, asking why is a central question, but not your why. You have to start with your listeners' why. Why do they listen? Why do they stop, if ever? Why you, when there are thousands of other podcasts on your topic? And is their why congruent with your why? Or do you have some more work to do?

There is no single why

The second aspect of why is to understand that there is no single reason why. There aren't infinite whys, or even an unmanageable number of them, but there are segments in your audience who listen (or could listen) to your show for multiple reasons, and those reasons are likely to be different. Humans are not monolithic. What's more, they don't always behave how we think they will.

My favorite example of this involves the toy My Little Pony. When Hasbro relaunched this property in 2010, the toys were accompanied by a media property (*My Little Pony: Friendship Is Magic*). The why at the time within Hasbro was probably something along the lines of "THOSE POWERPUFF GIRLS ARE EATING OUR LUNCH AT WALMART. WE NEED AN ANSWER!" Hasbro probably had a sales target of nine-year-old girls, and that informed its marketing and design choices.

But a funny thing happened when it paired the toys with the cartoon: it got multiple segments of customers buying its products, and each segment had its own distinct reason why. For the nine-year olds, it was to play along with the show, and maybe keep up with their friends. But the toy became hot with collectors as well, which led to another buying segment who were probably not girls and definitely not nine.

There was a third segment, though, that not even Hasbro could have predicted: a subculture of adult men who found the show's messages of friendship and compassion incredibly compelling, and even began to organize meetings where they would cosplay as various ponies and share stories of their appreciation for Twilight Sparkle. These "bronies" (bro ponies), as they were called, were not being ironic or cheeky; rather, they were sincere about the show's messaging and undercurrent of care. A female offshoot, the "pegasisters," also sprang up—again not as a joke, but as a sincere homage to the positivity the show embodied.

That's a why that I can assure you was not on the drawing board at Hasbro headquarters. Sometimes getting to the bottom of the various reasons why someone might gravitate towards your brand or offering takes a bit of digging, even for the most commodified products. Why do people buy scissors? To cut things. To cut what? Quilting squares. Why are you making a quilt? To leave a lasting gift for my daughter, who is getting married.

Oh! Now we are getting somewhere. What you discover when you keep asking "why" questions is that the real motivation behind any of our choices, from what to eat to what podcast we listen to, is driven by something below the surface, something beyond "it's interesting," if we just dig deep enough.

We will get to how we do that in the next episode, but before we get there, we have to talk about something that, like a trip to the dentist, you know you need to do but put off all the same: audience research.

The Myth of the Golden Gut

I started this book by asserting that knowing your audience was half (at least half) of crafting a successful podcast, and that almost no podcaster I have ever met puts even remotely that much effort into acquiring this knowledge. In my experience, there are two reasons for the reluctance of the average podcaster to dive into the arcane world of audience research. One is that they don't know how, or at least how to do it with limited resources. We are going to change all that in the next few episodes of this book.

The other reason is this prevailing wisdom that has risen at roughly the same time as a gradual devaluing of education and knowledge in American culture—that listening to advisers, research, and outside opinions just isn't what "mavericks" do. The models we currently have for entrepreneurialism are visionaries like Jeff Bezos, Elon Musk, and Richard Branson—outside-the-box thinkers who defied conventional wisdom, damned the torpedoes, and went full bore into their vision despite the naysayers around them. But for every Musk there are thousands of entrepreneurs who did the same thing and failed. They failed not because they weren't as smart (many most assuredly were) or because they weren't lucky (though Musk has certainly had his share of that). No, the number one reason they failed was that they made something the market didn't need or want, full stop.

This, I would submit, is also why most podcasters fail to break out of their immediate circle of family and friends. They made something the market didn't need or want, because they didn't ask the market.

The American automaker Henry Ford reportedly once said, "If I had asked people what they wanted, they would have said faster horses," and if I had a shiny nickel for every time someone has said that to or around me in the context of doing research, well, I would certainly have enough for a cold soda and maybe even a moving picture show.

There are three problems with Ford's quote and the interpretations thereof. First, there is no evidence Ford ever said this. Second, no competent market researcher in my profession would have reported to Ford that people wanted faster horses. My 1919 equivalent would have said that the kids want to see Grandma more, but it's a hard two-day ride from here and America can't get enough vacation time to spend so much time behind a buggy and maybe if we could get to Grandma in a few hours, we could see her more and Timmy could get some more of those Necco Wafer candies he loves so much.

The third thing I would say about this is that on the success of his "faster horse," the Model T, the Ford Motor Company had a two-thirds share of the American automobile industry in 1921. By 1926, after failing to respond to the market's desire for a more comfortable driving experience, that share had dropped to one-third. When the company finally introduced the Model A in 1927, Ford's market share was 15 percent. Maybe we can stop with the "faster horses" quote now.

But I recognize that entrepreneurial culture celebrates rogue thinkers—the ones who ignore the market and play their own game. Steve Jobs, as generational a rogue thinker as I've ever witnessed, once said that "people don't know what they want until you show it to them." That's certainly true. But that quote, and the sentiment behind it, has often been used as a justification for flat-out ignoring what people want in the service of a "vision" or the passion of a visionary entrepreneur. Not a day goes by when I don't see someone who should probably know better disparage surveys, market research, or consumer insights as the problem, and not the solution, to moribund products and services.

Take the broadcast radio industry, for instance. If you've listened to music radio lately, you'll note the following: localism is present mostly only in the advertising, playlists have been homogenized to utter blanditude (not a word, but should be), and the "personality" of a station has been delegated to prerecorded liners and jingles as the industry sends its "expensive" air talent packing. Often, when I read about the state of music radio on blogs, or see offhand remarks about radio on X/Twitter, I'll see people complain that stations have been "over-researched" into nondescript, banal jukeboxes—neither fish nor fowl.

Ironically, what these commenters don't know is that the radio industry, like other traditional media outlets, has never done less market research than it does today. In the mid-'90s, some of the most successful big-box radio stations spent a lot of money on local audience research—upwards of a quarter of a million dollars a year or more. Today, the average station is lucky to spend 10 percent of that, if anything, on learning what really matters to its listeners. So if you don't like the crap coming out of your speakers, don't blame research. Blame an industry with almost no ability or desire to listen to you. But I digress.

Equally damaging to the perception of market research is the opposite belief: that truly creative products and brands don't need to do research because they are shepherded by visionary leaders, like Jobs. The "myth of the golden gut" is often perpetuated by cult brands, which are eager to present themselves as driven by love, greatness, coolness, and any number of things that couldn't possibly have come from the clipboard of a market researcher. Apple is certainly one of those cult brands, and I've often seen its devotees celebrate the fact that it builds products with passion and not with surveys.

This perception couldn't be further from the truth. In fact, market research has always been an important part of Apple's product strategy. Back in 2010, I watched Jobs give one of his famous product announcement keynotes—this time for the new line of iPods, which included a redesigned Shuffle (a minimalist, screenless audio player) and a new Nano, the smallest iPod with a screen. The clues were all there—this line of iPods was heavily influenced by market research. Yes, it takes a creative genius like Jonathan Ive to translate consumer needs into brushed aluminum and a visionary leader like Jobs to set the standards for his product team almost impossibly high. If you watch the speech, however, you'll hear a dozen references to Apple's consumer research efforts and how that research was an integral part of Apple's iPod lineup.

A few examples: The 2010 iPod Shuffle saw the return of buttons, which Jobs attributed to listening to customers and their desire to return to the more obvious control scheme of earlier Shuffles. True, the previous buttonless model didn't sell very well, which is in itself a form of information, but were that their only source of data, they would have just killed it and not returned it to the control scheme of an earlier version.

The new Nano was a product of both listening to consumer requests to make it smaller and continued consumer research into the most popular use cases for the Nano. It was no accident that the new iteration had a built-in clip, or that the Nike+ app was mentioned and highlighted in Jobs's description of it; Apple knew through its market research that exercise was one of the key drivers for Nano usage, and it optimized the device accordingly. Jobs himself said it over and over—we listened to our customers. If you think that meant Jobs got a few cranky emails and decided to change a billion-dollar product line out of sheer whim, well, you'd be the exact opposite of right.

Finally, if you've shopped in an Apple Store, you have probably gotten a follow-up survey about your Apple Store experience. I've gotten four or five and have dutifully filled out every one. The next time you have a subpar experience in an Apple Store and you don't fill out your follow-up survey, you become that guy. You know, the one who complains about the government but never votes. That guy.

So, as romantic as the "golden gut" notion is, it just doesn't hold up in practice. In fact, the interwebs are littered with companies that were visionary, wildly creative, and challenged the status quo to make something truly great—and failed.

I will give you the most obvious manifestation of this—something all of us have said at one time or another, when someone didn't "get" what we were trying to accomplish or achieve with a given creative effort: "I don't understand why they aren't getting it/this isn't working/they don't like it."

I call this the Bon Jovi Problem. Bon Jovi has sold over 50 million albums—a remarkable achievement. I'm not a huge fan; you might not be either. In fact, when I tell people this fact, they will often respond in the same way: "I don't understand how Bon Jovi could sell 50 million albums." As a music fan, I can understand this sentiment. As an audience researcher, however, I hear this completely differently. I hear this as "I don't understand 50 million people."

And that, my friends, is a pretty damning admission to make if you are in the business of entertaining humans. To entertain the humans, you have to understand the humans first. Understanding Bon Jovi comes later. If that's even possible. Dude bought an Arena Football League team. But I can tell you this—50 million people aren't wrong. Nobody understands their audience like John Francis Bongiovi Jr.

The Cycle of Insight

At the beginning of this book, I promised you that I would teach you a process I call the Cycle of Insight. The process is simple: it involves alternating between doing qualitative research and quantitative research until either a) you are satisfied with the growth of your podcast, or b) the sun burns out, whichever comes first. Here's what it looks like:

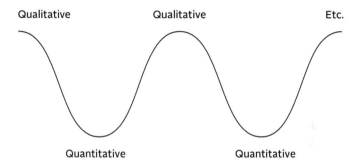

The word "etc." is doing the heavy lifting here. You see, the Cycle of Insight is a process that should *never* end, as long as your podcast is still going. Your audience is changing every day—sometimes because new people are replacing older listeners, which changes the character of your audience, and sometimes because the people themselves change. There's no better example of that than the way media habits were completely thrown for a loop by the COVID-19 lockdowns. THAT was a wacky time for audio and video, let me tell you. People stopped commuting (and listening to AM/FM radio in the car), and instead, we all watched *Tiger King* on Netflix. Even today, with the lockdowns well in our rearview mirrors, media habits are not exactly the same as they were at the beginning of 2020.

While the process may have no end, it most assuredly has a beginning. Alternating between qualitative and quantitative approaches, we are going to drill down, in order, through four essential questions:

1   *Why* would someone listen (or not listen) to your show? (Qualitative)

2   *Who* are the people who share those reasons, and who are they at home? (Quantitative)

3   *How* do those audience segments want to be reached? (Qualitative)

4   *What* are the topics, benchmarks, guests, and elements that appeal to each segment? (Quantitative)

Before we go on, I need to answer the question in the room: What is qualitative and quantitative research, and what is the difference between them? Part of the answer is in the four points above—qualitative research is talking to people to understand *why* and *how* they do things, while quantitative research is best for describing and counting *who* would do those things and *what* the things are. More specifically, though, here are the key differences.

Qualitative research

While metrics and numbers give us a snapshot of who's tuning in, they rarely tell the full story. Enter qualitative research, the unsung hero for podcasters aiming to delve deeper into the psyche of their listeners.

Think of qualitative research as your personal guide through the dense forest of audience understanding. While quantitative research provides the *what*—how many listeners tuned in, skipped, or subscribed—qualitative research illuminates the *why*. Why did a particular segment resonate? Why do listeners prefer one format over another? It's akin to having a heart-to-heart with your audience, minus the studio mics and editing.

But qualitative research is not merely about asking questions; it's about asking the right questions. By diving into the world of qualitative insights, podcasters can transform their content from merely being heard to being deeply felt and understood. This is not just about filling airtime; it's about filling a space in your listener's day, their conversations, and perhaps even their hearts. The key is to remember that it's not just the numbers that speak; sometimes, the most profound insights come from the silent pauses, the emotive feedback, and the shared stories of your audience.

The term sounds fancy, and yes, there is a whole world of focus groups and ethnographic research (watching people in their natural environment) that costs money and time, and podcasters have little of either. But really, qualitative research is little more than having conversations with listeners—not asking them multiple-choice questions, but talking to them and getting to know them, either through email, in person, or in a forum or other discussion group. The goal of qualitative is never to find "the answer." You would have to talk to a *lot* of people to get that! The goal is to get language and ideas for possible answers, which you can test further in quantitative research.

Quantitative research

While heart-to-heart conversations and listener feedback give us the soulful beats of our show, numbers and metrics provide the rhythm, ensuring we stay in tune with our audience's desires.

Imagine quantitative research, dear podcasters, as the backstage tech crew of a grand theater production. They might not be under the spotlight, but without their precise measures and attention to detail, the show wouldn't go on. This kind of research isn't just about counting how many ears heard your latest episode. It's about tracking trends over time, identifying peak engagement moments, and recognizing patterns. Did a guest appearance spike your downloads? Was there a drop in listeners halfway through a series? Quantitative research offers these insights with clear, undeniable data.

Don't underestimate the power of numbers. While the soul of podcasting might lie in storytelling and connection, its pulse is very much driven by the metrics. Embracing quantitative research doesn't mean sacrificing the heart of your content. Instead, think of it as giving your podcast a checkup, ensuring it's healthy, thriving, and reaching the vast potential of listeners eager for your next episode.

The "cycle" part of this is that when you conduct this kind of research, generally in the form of a listener survey, you are going to be left with some more questions along with those answers. You may wonder why 26 percent of your audience hated this segment, or why they haven't recommended your show to a friend. And this means going back to qualitative research (even to conversations you've already had, looking for different things) to learn the answers.

Listener surveys don't have to cost a dime. While there are paid tools you can use, like Qualtrics or SurveyMonkey, there are also low- or no-cost alternatives, ranging from things like Typeform to a simple Google Form, which will accomplish most, if not all, of what you want to do.

How do you choose?

In the grand symphony of crafting content, there are moments that call for the soft nuances of a violin and times when the bold strokes of a drum make more sense. Similarly, in the realm of research, there's a dance between quantitative and qualitative approaches. Understanding when to let one lead over the other can dramatically influence the success of your show.

When should you let the structured beats of quantitative research guide you? Opt for this when you're looking to validate a hypothesis or need hard numbers. Say you've launched a new segment and you're curious if it's hitting the mark. Quantitative research gives you clear metrics— what percentage of listeners liked it, what turned them off, and how this episode's stats compare with others. It's about broad strokes, trends, and measurable outcomes. Numbers might seem cold, but they often present the clearest picture of where you stand and what adjustments are needed.

On the other hand, the rich melodies of qualitative research are perfect when you're looking for depth and understanding. It's less about "How many?" and more about "Why?" or "How?" If you're pondering the nuances of your listener's experience, or want to dive deep into their emotions and motivations, this is your go-to. Imagine you want to know *why* a particular episode resonated so well, or *how* listeners truly feel about a controversial topic you covered. Here, one-on-one interviews, open-ended questions, or focus group discussions can be gold mines.

In the journey of podcasting, it's not an either-or decision. The duet between quantitative and qualitative research can be truly harmonious. Start with qualitative insights to form theories, use numbers to identify trends and test those theories, and then go back to qualitative insights to add depth and context and the rationale behind those quantitative results. For a podcaster, this means beginning with simple conversations, however you can have them, and then using a simple listener survey to see how many people share the same opinions, and what else they might have in common. That's really all there is to it! The key is not to expect answers from qualitative or insight from quantitative. Using both, in concert (I'll stop with the music analogy now), in a repeated cycle, is the key to audience *mastery*.

In our next episode, we are going to start where I suggest you start: with qualitative insights about your audience. And cake. Trust me, the next episode goes well with cake.

Episode Three
What We Talk about When We Talk about Podcasts

Betty Crocker

My ultimate goal is to get you to field a listener survey, with as many responses as you can possibly get. But first, I want you to talk to six listeners. Twelve would be better, and twenty would be awesome, but let's start with six.

What can six listeners tell you? How can you possibly trust the responses from so few? Well, six people aren't going to give you the right answers. But they are going to help you ask better questions, because you can write the questions you will ask in a survey to test whether or not the "why" insights those listeners give you are shared by others—and you can ask those questions in the language of the listeners, instead of with your own biases and the "curse of knowledge" you have about your own show.

A small number of listeners can tell you all kinds of things in an in-depth conversation that are at least true for them, and those individual truths will lead you to write a listener survey to see if others think the same way, and how best to reach them. If you think of qualitative research as listener brainstorming rather than "research," you will have the right mindset, because approaching it with an open mind will lead you to insights that no survey ever could.

I'll give you one of the best examples I know of this. There is an apocryphal story in the annals of market research that I particularly love, about cake mix. ("Apocryphal," by the way, is Greek for "a pile of crap," so this probably isn't true—but I'll tell the story anyway.)

The story goes that back in the '50s, Betty Crocker had developed its first completely one-box cake mix: just add water and bake. After some initial buzz, sales began to disappoint, so the Betty Crocker executives did a series of focus groups to suss out the problem.

Imagine tackling this problem today, using social media monitoring or tracking clickstream behavior. Betty Crocker might observe fewer clicks to its recipe page or perhaps fewer positive mentions. Coupon activity from register scans might decline. Positive sentiment for Duncan Hines might increase. We might learn that the best time to tweet about cakes is 10:00 a.m. on a Sunday. Maybe we'd record an increase in the number of tweets about the poor quality of Betty Crocker's mix. We could take all this online behavior—all these tweets and clicks—and determine a few things. Some of our conclusions would be correct, while others would be off the mark. Mining this information is crucial to the lifeblood of the organization, don't get me wrong. But bits and bytes will only ever tell you the *what*. They rarely give you the straight story on the *why*.

One thing I've learned in twenty-five years of doing qualitative research is that people are not as expressive about products and services and shows as we'd like them to be. Often, we cannot clearly articulate what makes us uncomfortable or dissatisfied with a given product, so we fall back on the easy answers: "It doesn't taste right." "It costs too much." "I don't have enough time."

These are the first things I hear in any focus group, before Stockholm syndrome really sets in. This is when the experienced qualitative researcher reaches into their bag of tricks and helps the respondents along—and uncovers the real reasons behind these perceptions of quality, value, and importance. These data, of course, are anecdotal until you can test the underlying assumptions, and social media is providing us with more and more tools to do just that. But social media often gives us the easy answers—not the true answers.

Back to Betty Crocker. Unable to mine Twitter (X!), our 1950s executives did a series of focus groups with housewives who had tried and ultimately rejected their cake mix. Much to their surprise, they realized that these ladies thought the cakes tasted just fine and were pretty good value. Instead, the insight they developed over time was that the cake mixes were a little too *easy*. In postwar America, as their husbands worked long days, these stay-at-home moms were a little embarrassed about the fact that all they had to do to have a delicious cake on the table for their men to enjoy after work was just add water and stir. In short, they felt guilty.

This is why you now have to add an egg, or perhaps a little oil, to a cake mix. Certainly, these ingredients could be incorporated into the package—we do have a little history of food science in this country. But adding these one or two ingredients made it feel like *baking* again and not assembling. These women didn't just want cakes—they wanted to feel good.

The numbers only give you half the story—and I say this as someone who makes his living telling the stories of numbers. The operative word there, of course, is "story." It's easy to be seduced by social media data, especially by those who loudly proclaim that they have the numbers on their side. Numbers aren't on anyone's side. I've had a lifelong battle with them, trust me. Adding insights to data is more than just putting flesh on the bones of an otherwise solid skeleton. Often, you don't know what you think you know merely by dredging tweets. You have to talk to the people, and see how they react, before you can really understand their motivations enough to then test them out in a survey.

Five Great Questions

Now, you might think that you know your audience a little bit better than the Betty Crocker executives knew theirs. You certainly aren't as far removed from them as the (likely) roomful of white male executives in the '50s making decisions about the (mostly) women who were buying their product. But you have got to be open to this process, and keep an open mind. Here's why.

The biggest lie we podcasters all tell ourselves is this: "I know my audience." Let me assure you, unless your audience consists solely of friends and family (and we've all been there), you do not know your audience. I could spend five minutes with you, quizzing you about the habits and beliefs and values of your audience, and stump you with basics every single time. Heck, I could stump myself about the *Sounds Profitable* podcast audience the same way! We are all fighting a great battle.

I've spent twenty-five years studying the care and feeding of an audience, and I'll be the first to admit that I don't always understand what works and what doesn't. It's a practice—a discipline—to incorporate the voice of the listener into every single thing that we do. For my larger network clients, this often takes the form of listener surveys and other formal research projects. But I have to be honest here—even at the highest levels of podcasting, not enough of this work is being done to truly understand the most important thing you can know about the audience: why they chose your show and, more importantly, why they would recommend it to a friend. Instead, most of the work is about understanding the listener as product, the thing that we bundle and sell to advertisers.

If that sounds cynical, I don't mean it to be so. Advertiser-focused research is what is paying the bills for all of us in the ad-supported world, and the bills need to be paid before we can invest in content research and other flights of fancy. Advertisers want to know the age, gender, and income of your audience. They want to know if they have kids, and a 401(k), and an aging car, and an expiring phone contract. But none of those advertiser-focused things—NONE of them—will help your show get *better*.

So what will? More importantly, how can podcasters with limited resources learn more about their audience and what makes them tick? Crazy thought here: you can talk to them. I am not talking about an audience survey or conducting focus groups or anything like that. Just talk to them. Let them know in your show itself that you'd love to open a dialogue with them, and learn more about why they listen, what keeps them coming back, and what you could do to improve. This can take the form of an email, a Slack channel, a Google Form, or, yes, even a survey. As long as you open a dialogue, you are doing the work.

But here is the issue—we don't always know the right questions to ask. After conducting hundreds of focus groups with tens of thousands of humans all over the world, I can assure you that if you ask a listener what they think of your podcast, the answer will be "I dunno—I like it. It's pretty good. It's funny/interesting." Super helpful, right?

The reality is that humans (especially American humans) have access to a much greater vocabulary for what they don't like than for what they do. With a generic question like "What do you think of my podcast?" you are likely to get a very generic positive answer. It's when we don't like something that we gain access to a more specific lexicon.

So, what do we talk about when we talk about our podcasts? The key to generating insight is to avoid questions that are hypothetical, abstract, or general (HAG) in favor of those that are specific, actual, and personal (SAP). These are really awful acronyms, my apologies (RAAMA).

Five (plus) great questions

So here are some great questions you can ask your listeners that will genuinely help you understand them better, and thus serve them better. I have shared these at conferences with audiences all over the world, and now I share them with you.

1　How did you discover my show?

Often, when we ask this in listener surveys, it is for marketing purposes—what channels are more effective in terms of promoting the show, and which ones should I spend less time on? This is all helpful information, but I prefer to ask this question to understand the exact transaction or negotiation that occurred at the moment of discovery, and not to learn which channel to invest more heavily in. After all, the top means of discovery in podcasting continues to be recommendations from friends and family, and we are not about to increase our "friends and family" budget.

Instead, I like to get down to the actual moment, if the listener can remember it. Was it a recommendation? What was the context for that? What information did you give the recommender, and how did they then "sell" the show to you? If you were searching for a show, what exactly *were* you searching for? Did you get it? Again: specific, actual, and personal. These kinds of questions probably work best in an actual conversation or video call, but I bet you have listeners who would be thrilled to do this with you.

2 **What other podcasts do you listen to?**

This is another question often used for marketing purposes (where can I run promos?) that is actually more important for insight. When I ask this question, I am trying to get to the heart of the consideration set of the listener, and where my show slots in. Is my sports podcast the only sports podcast they listen to? Why is that? Is it one of five? Why do they bother, and what does my show give them that the rest do not? What I am trying to discover here, as James Joyce asks in *Ulysses*, is "Who's he when he's at home?"

Understanding the full media diet of your listener, and where exactly your show slots in, is the key to leaving deeper footprints with an audience. Sometimes it is in the vocabulary of other things they listen to that a listener gains the language to describe what your show is, or is not.

3 **Would you make the show shorter or longer?**

This is an excellent way to turn a lousy question ("How long should my podcast be?") into an insight-generating question. A listener cannot tell you how long your podcast should be. That isn't their job. They might give you an *answer*, but it won't be particularly valuable. But asking about making the show shorter or longer is an entrée to a better question: What would you cut or do less of? (if the answer is shorter), or What would you like to enjoy more of? (if the answer is longer). These are things the listener can talk about intelligently and in a way that is actionable for you. Anyway, the answer to the "How long should my podcast be?" question, one of the crappiest questions of all time, is this: "Shorter than your last one!"

4 Think about a friend or family member who would like this show—and tell me about them!

(This one is a bit of a two-parter, but if you only have time to talk to someone about one thing, I'd recommend a variation of it.) Who are they, what do they look like, what do they do for a living, and why would you make this recommendation? That's all part one. Part two is the logical conclusion: *Describe the show for that person.* What would you highlight, and why? The key here, again, is to push beyond the abstract and aggregate to learn as much as you possibly can about this specific real human, and the specific way your listener would talk about your show to them, right down to inside jokes and other shared experiences. The more detail you can elicit here, the more insight you will have into how people really think about what it is you are doing. They may highlight a strength of yours that you weren't really considering. They also might "apologize" to their friend for something they don't really care for about the show but that is overshadowed by positive things you do.

Getting people to imagine a specific, actual human who would like the show, and how they would pitch the show to that human, is the key to getting the vocabulary you might use to pitch the show to larger audiences yourself. Some of the most powerful brands in media have made these kinds of insights key to their DNA. Think back to the example of Taco Bell and its evolution from "fresh." But why do we eat at Taco Bell today? Because it's late and we are drunk or high. Look at its marketing now. The glistening heads of lettuce are gone, replaced by Dorito-encrusted Mountain Dew chalupas. Because they realized the thing that we already knew—it's late, and we're drunk.

5   **If this show were to die tomorrow—never be produced again—what one thing, if any, would you miss?**

This is the question I like to end any focus group with. I call it "the eulogy question." Now, I want to warn you here that the answer might well be "nothing." That's a problem, and you need to know it. But people are more articulate in describing loss than gain. They might tell you that your show "is good, it's funny," but take that same show away and you are likely to get a very specific thing, and maybe one that you hadn't considered as core to your show.

I'll give you an example from my own listening. I listen to multiple episodes of *The Ryen Russillo Podcast* every week—every one he puts out. It's a sports podcast, and if you were to ask me what I like about it, I could certainly talk about his reasoned and enlightened takes on sports, his different perspectives on the business of sports, and his guests. But if that show were taken away from me? My eulogy would talk about one thing and one thing only: "Life Advice." At the end of every show, Ryen takes listener emails from (largely) Gen Z and millennial males who are looking for advice on their real-life problems and need either a dad, a big brother, or just a referee to help adjudicate disputes with their friends. Ryen serves here as the dad/big brother who's been through it, while "producer Kyle" sits in as the younger voice of the audience. It's deftly done, wildly entertaining, and works on multiple levels. Take that away and the show would still be good, but I would mourn the loss of "Life Advice" more than any sports content on the show.

Make It Worthwhile

Those five(-plus) questions provide a solid foundation for engaging with your audience about your show. This process isn't quantitative research, it's qualitative, but the insights gathered can be tested later via surveys. The feedback you seek doesn't require validation from hundreds of listeners. If you receive similar comments from several people, it's worth considering what they have to say about your show.

This is an informal process, so start collecting feedback now. Don't wait for a tool or a perfect process—just start engaging listeners, even by email. Understanding why people listen to (or stop listening to) your show is invaluable, and the best way to truly understand the potential reasons for this is to ask real-life questions to real people in real situations. Most importantly, remember to *listen*.

Whether you are talking to listeners in a conversation or formally surveying them (as we will soon discuss), it's crucial to make answering these questions worthwhile for your listeners. Consider rewarding their participation with swag, exclusive content, or special access. After all, by choosing to respond, they're showing a deeper connection with your show. Moreover, when you've had these conversations and implemented changes, acknowledge that the show's improvements are due to the audience's input. Whether you're introducing something new or removing something old, thank your listeners for helping you make those decisions.

The feel-good reason to do this is that it's the right thing to do, at whatever scale you can manage, to make your listeners feel they are part of a community and not just being talked at. The selfish reason, however, is to improve your response rates, especially when we get to actually fielding your own survey. A survey that no one takes is not a very good survey. The key is to treat all these interactions like any other social interaction—you can't just take, take, take. You gotta give. This is the kind of thing that any number of companies that should know better screw up all the time—and it really takes very little to make people feel valued.

I'll give you a great example. This is for an online survey, but I want you to think about these things even when you are just talking to a handful of listeners in a qualitative setting. I once got an invitation to take an online survey sent to me from a market research company on behalf of a leading jeweler. The name of the jeweler isn't important—let's just say it is a reassuringly expensive store that rhymes with "Spiffany." I got this survey because I've made online purchases with this retailer and am thus on its mailing list.

What struck me about this particular survey solicitation was the value it placed on my feedback: none. Sure, there was a perfunctory "thank you for taking the survey" line in there, but no actual incentive for me to take part. There's nothing remarkable about that fact; indeed, it's all too common for us to get survey requests that offer no incentives. It's why we associate online surveys with "quick and cheap." But as the sign above my dry cleaner says: *Quality, Service or Price—Pick Any Two.*

I thought a lot about this particular solicitation, and I think there are lessons here for ANYONE who solicits feedback from their customers or audience.

Here's the problem as far as this particular survey is concerned. Yes, they will get responses. There are, however, some pretty significant biases with these responses that folks in my profession call "non-response bias." The first, of course, is the unknowable unknown of how many Spiffany customers just wouldn't take *any* web survey— and what their buying habits are. This is true of any online survey and especially true of one with no incentive. And what you don't know are the differences between those who would take such a survey and those who would not.

Using our Spiffany example, how much more (or less) likely are consumers who buy $20,000 rings to take an online survey than customers who just bought a ceramic Dalmatian? (*Wheel of Fortune*, circa 1984—the LAST PRIZE YOU BUY.)

I'm going to make an assumption here (and yes, it is an assumption, but the point is that you can't prove it right or wrong without doing the work): customers who are in the top quintile of spending are less likely to take an online survey than customers in the lower tier of spending. Or vice versa. Or you don't know. But that's the point. If we assume the former to be true, however, then sending a survey with no incentive and no reward for completion is likely to overrepresent lower-tier purchasers.

In fact, Spiffany's very customer database could be overrepresented by not-so-big spenders. I've made two purchases with this particular retailer. The first was for about $250. A trinket! A mere bauble! I confidently entered my credit card information online and awaited the UPS truck. The second thing I purchased was engagement-ring expensive, which required (in my case) some reassuring human contact. I made this purchase in the store, where I was not asked to provide my email address—and thus, this purchase is not connected to their online survey database.

All of that said, I was in their database, and they did send me a survey. Take this 20-minute survey, they said, and, umm, we will appreciate it. At a personal level, I felt devalued. It wouldn't take much to show me that they truly valued my opinion. But asking me to do their work for them, for free, after dropping the chunk of change I've spent with them? The temerity! No, the more I spend with them, the more I want them to convince me that not only my business but also my feedback is valuable. (By the way, lest the folks at Spiffany think I've picked on them, let me just say this: The blue bag. It's magic. Trust me on this one.)

Of course, cash is the king of incentives, but if you have any sort of relationship with your listeners, you don't have to go that far. You just have to show them that they matter. It could be merch, or access to exclusive content, or a higher status on your Discord or Patreon community, or even just a mention on the show. In doing that, you've gone beyond merely providing me with an incentive to take your survey—you've strengthened my loyalty to the show, period.

One more thing about soliciting feedback from your audience: don't just collect and forget! As you sift through the data you are going to collect about your show, you are going to make some changes, and you are going to want to communicate those changes to your audience. Continue to tell them, long after you've asked your questions, that everything you are doing to make the show better is a result of talking to *them*—you value their feedback and you are doing something with it, not just filing it away.

If you value your listeners at the start of the process and then acknowledge their input at the end, you will create a virtuous circle between the desire to share information *with* your show and the desire to spread information *about* your show to others.

Episode Four
The Listener Survey

How to Field a DIY Listener Survey

Once you have spent some time in written or verbal conversations with some of your listeners, you are ready to start putting together some hypotheses about what makes your show tick and what could be better. Remember that what we are looking for from the previous step are the reasons why someone might listen or not listen to your show. We aren't judging these reasons yet—we need to test them out first.

I will provide a sample listener survey at the end of this episode to get you started, but your goal with this survey is to figure out the "who" behind the whys. How many people share the same reasons why they like or don't like the show? Can we combine groups of people into segments that represent large sections of your audience? What else do those people do with their time—what other podcasts do they listen to, when do they listen to them, and how does your show fit into their other sources of entertainment and information?

Certainly, if your show has repeatable segments or benchmarks, you are going to want to get a read on their appeal relative to each other; you might even want to probe reactions to notable guests or even the host(s) themselves. The qualitative phase should have left you with a lot of questions, and those questions should generally start with the same phrase: "I wonder if… " The listener survey is your chance to satisfy that curiosity. Basically, any question about which you "wonder if" it's true or not should go into your survey.

It's also the time to ask some questions about what else your listeners do when they aren't listening to your podcast—what do they read, what do they watch, what do they listen to? The answers to these questions deepen your understanding of your audience, of course, but they also tell you where you might be able to find like-minded new listeners for your podcast and suggest ways to reach them as well.

Best Practices

There is nothing scary about fielding your own listener survey, but there are some pitfalls to watch out for. You don't have to be a professional researcher to get feedback from your audience—but there are good ways and not-so-good ways to do so, and I want you to do good. My intent here is to give you A Pretty Good Start, which coincidentally is also the name of my two-star daycare franchise.

Since many of these thoughts are driven by the questions I most often get from podcasters, I thought I would structure this like an FAQ. Here we go.

Why do I need a listener survey?

I'll give you two reasons. First, listener surveys are a crucial part of attracting sponsors, if that is your thing. If your goal is to monetize your podcast, then you have to get your head around the fact that the product you are selling is your audience, and your sponsors have a right to know what they are buying. Nothing more needs to be said about that, I hope.

Most of us, however, aren't trying to monetize our shows—but we would like to make them *better*. Here's a thing I believe: podcasting is one of the hardest crafts to level up. You can go from awful to competent at a reliable pace, but how do you go from competent to *great*? There are a lot of hard truths wrapped up in that, but one component is, absolutely, audience feedback. You may harbor a romantic vision that your art transcends understanding, like Edvard Munch's famous painting *The Scream*. But prior to painting *The Scream*, Munch painted a terrible picture of his neighbor's dog, and I can guarantee you someone "gave him feedback" about that. We can always do better.

Your listeners (not your family and friends) are the most reliable way to find out if your baby is ugly, and that is the first step towards building a great show. Accepting feedback from your audience is sometimes difficult and sometimes counterintuitive, *but it is the only way to master the craft*.

When *shouldn't* I field a listener survey?

If you have a very small audience (a few hundred or less), I wouldn't work on a formal survey just yet. Those early few listeners are incredibly valuable to you, and yes, you should find ways to talk to them, whether that is by email or on social media. But *conversations* like the kind we covered in Episode Three are better tools for the job until you start to get both core AND casual listeners.

Successful media properties, including podcasts, have three layers of audiences: there are *primary* listeners, who never miss an episode and can quote every inside joke; *secondary* listeners, who will look at the topic that week before deciding to listen; and a *tertiary* layer of listeners, who might listen once a month or so when they run out of other shows or are stuck too long in traffic. All these layers are part of a healthy audience strategy. In the early days of your podcast, your audience is probably weighted more towards primary listeners—you may even know most of them—but when you start to get casual listeners, that's when you know it's time to think about a survey, because you now have the makings of your first line of inquiry as a podcaster: How can I convert occasional listeners to regular listeners?

Focusing too soon on the handful of early listeners might help you craft Mom's Favorite Podcast, but you run the risk of falling into a trap by focusing too soon on an early, tiny core and ignoring the potentially greener pastures you could graze in in the future. If you can, seek out someone whose opinion you trust, who has had some success in podcasting, and who is willing to listen to your show and give some honest feedback.

So... conversations, not statistics. Once you start to have a really layered audience, then it's time to entertain a listener survey.

What kinds of questions should I ask?

I wrote a bunch for you at the end of this episode. Fret not.

How long should my survey be?

Since you are going to be prevailing on the good graces of your listeners to take this survey, your prime directive is to keep it as brutally short as possible. It's better to fire off multiple, mercifully short surveys in the service of differing goals than it is to field one honkin' big survey that only fifty people complete. So, if you aren't really going to do anything with questions like "What is your company size?" or "How many hours per day do you use the internet?" leave 'em out. Your survey should focus only on the actionable information you absolutely need, and the minimum classification data (demographics/psychographics) you need to make sense of it. No more.

Can you give me any advice on writing my own questions?

Okay—this is a big topic, but it's super important. Writing a good questionnaire is an art as much as it is a science. One basic tenet is that your sequence of questioning, like that of a good trial lawyer, shouldn't lead your witness by introducing facts not in evidence. This means that if you ask a specific question early on about Spotify, don't be surprised if a later question that asks respondents to name podcast platforms they use reports a high percentage of Spotify users—you've planted the suggestion.

Start with the most general, basic questions and leave questions about specifics until the very end. You might think about it like this: start by asking respondents open-ended questions (fill-in-the-blank, not multiple-choice) about the podcasts they listen to, then ask consistent questions about the shows the respondents named in general, and finally, close by asking specific questions about specific podcasts, named or not.

Of course, using open-ended questions (in which the respondents write in their answers, instead of selecting from a list of options) creates extra work for you. For each such question you ask, you are going to have to go into each completed survey and code every open-ended response, normalizing "FB" into "Facebook" and "Bill Simmons" into "The Bill Simmons Podcast" so that you can make sense of the results. Yes, it's work. That's what makes it worth doing.

The alternative is to ask multiple-choice questions, but know that the danger with these is failing to provide enough options. A question about which smartphone a respondent uses might get away with a handful of choices: a) Apple iPhone, b) Android, c) BlackBerry (pour one out for BlackBerry), etc. A question with a greater potential range of answers, however, will be problematic. If your choices aren't extensive enough to cover the vast majority of possible answers, you're likely to get either a lot of unusable "Other" responses or, worse, the Stockholm syndrome–inflicted condition whereby the beleaguered respondent tires of hunting for the "best" answer and just selects the first choice on the page. That, my friends, is useless. So give your respondents lots of choices on multiple-choice questions, or use open-ended (fill-in-the-blank) questions where you have doubts.

End your survey with demographic/classification questions. These questions (age/gender/income, etc.) work best at the end because they are simple and quick—and, as researchers have determined over the years, placing them at the end of the survey is a best practice for getting people to finish your survey, which is pretty important. It's best if you keep your classification system consistent with the same gold standard we pros use: the US (or whatever your country of origin is) census.

What kind of tools do I need?

Listener feedback can be as simple as asking people to email you. You don't need expensive software. On the free end, most people won't need anything more than Google Forms to field a simple survey. You can also spend a little on tools like Typeform or SurveyMonkey. Obviously, in my research career, I have used some fairly expensive tools that pack quite a bit of horsepower, but you don't need those kinds of tools if you keep your survey short and simple. If you are using a free tool, here is a good rule of thumb: if what you are asking for is too complex for the tool to handle, don't ask for it. Do a simpler thing. You must challenge your listeners, not defeat them.

How do I get people to take my survey?

Now we come to a meaty topic! For most people, the sole driver of survey responses is going to be asking people to take the survey in the flow of your podcast itself. Given that the live, in-podcast solicitation is going to be the main driver for people to take your survey, put your back into it! First, make it easy to find. Wherever your questionnaire is hosted, get a short, easy-to-remember link that redirects to it. The best practice for your show is to have your own URL and website, which makes it easy for you to make a page on the site called Survey that just redirects to wherever your survey is hosted (e.g., http://www.yourpodcast.com/survey). This is simple to do with WordPress, Squarespace, or Wix sites. Don't make your listeners have to think or spell.

For the solicitation itself, tell people *why* you are doing it and how important it is to the show. Sell it! I have conducted numerous cross-network surveys for large podcast networks in which I've combined surveys for each show, weighted to download numbers along with other associated data, to come up with demographic and psychographic profiles for the network and for each podcast. Once, we did this across a particularly large podcast network that featured some BIG shows (certainly Top 50) and a variety of much smaller shows. One of those smaller shows, a *very* niche podcast, completely *killed* it compared with larger shows in terms of survey responses because they didn't just say, "Oh, take our survey," at the end of the show. They actually *wrote, performed, and produced an original song* that encouraged people to take the survey. Let me tell you, people took that survey.

Do you need to work that hard? No. But could you, to great effect? This is between you and your god. In any case, you'll get the best results if the host(s) talk about the survey in an engaged, passionate way. You *want* people to give their feedback, so act the part.

And, as we discussed in the last episode, think through what kind of incentive you could offer to show people how much you value and appreciate their feedback. Consider why people listen to your show and how you could give them *more* of that. An exclusive tool or piece of content. Have a fantasy sports show? Give survey takers access to your custom player valuations. Fashion podcast? The ten most essential pieces for your wardrobe. A new car buyers' guide. Tips to beat your neighbors in *Among Us*. A character guide and maps for your fiction podcast. A custom bodyweight workout routine for your fitness podcast. Do some work, for Pete's sake. This says more than "I value your time." It says, "I value *you*."

Should I also ask for survey responses on social media or on my website?

In the quest for completed surveys, you may be tempted to promote the survey everywhere you can: social media, your website, etc. Resist this urge if you can. You see the best results when the sample is pure and driven solely by people responding to an audio solicitation in the podcast itself. You know you are getting *listeners* then, at least. Whenever clients insist that they want to promote the survey across X/Twitter or to their company email database, we make sure we can distinguish those responses from the ones driven by the podcast itself. Responses from social can be especially wonky compared with other sources.

You at least want to be able to tell them apart, so use different survey links.

If you have an email database that was solely developed from and for the podcast, that is an exception to the previous advice. If you don't, now you have yet another good reason to build one. Email is still the milkshake that brings all the people to the yard.

How long should I run the survey?

I'd recommend talking about the survey for at least three episodes. Depending on the level of engagement of your audience, this should be sufficient to make most people aware that you are looking for their feedback. My wonderful former boss Frank Cody used to characterize the magic of three as "Huh? What? Ohhh... " The first time you mention it, people will barely be aware that you've made an ask. The second, they'll crane their heads forward a bit, just to see what they missed. The third time is the charm. So I would hit the survey hard for three episodes, and then give it a rest. You don't want the survey solicitations to become wallpaper—and you may want to repeat your efforts in a year—so don't make the survey a throwaway tag at the end of every show. There is a reason why pledge drives work in public radio a lot better than just asking for money every single day.

How many people do I need to make it statistically reliable?

At last, we come to the most FA'd FAQ I ever hear. I'm going to tell you something that will either disappoint you or give you great relief: your survey will not be statistically representative of your audience. In a previous life, I worked on the national election exit polling for the major news networks. For that effort, we had to take great pains to ensure that in every precinct we sampled, we weren't just taking questionnaires from the people who approached us; we approached a consistent pattern of voters and recorded their responses, non-responses, and demographic information, whether they participated or not. With this information, we could weight the exit poll data and calibrate it to prior voting/registration patterns within a margin of error.

That type of sampling is called "probabilistic sampling"—every voter in the precinct has an equal, non-zero chance of being included. Your listener survey has no way to deal with non-response bias—it is what we call "self-selected" sampling. The margin of error for a self-selected study is "yes." Instead, the key metrics for you to focus on are sample quality and response rate. If you field a study about your fantasy sports podcast and you get two million responses from non-sports fans, your results are probably crap. On the other hand, if your podcast is pitched to high-level CMOs and you get ten Fortune 100 CMOs to take your survey, you'd be okay with a sample of ten. That's the sample quality aspect.

Response rate is the other key variable. We typically don't look at anything under 100 persons, and of course more is more gooder. More important, however, is the relationship between that sample and the size of your downloads. If your show gets 1,000 downloads per episode, a 100-person sample would be pretty incredible! If your show gets 50,000 downloads, however, 100 persons would not be a great response rate, and a sign that you might need to go back to the drawing board to revamp your solicitation. If you can get 5 percent of your estimated audience to respond, you are doing extremely well indeed. Remember that you don't just want your superfans to respond—you need those more casual listeners. (Again, an incentive of some kind will help with this.)

Finally, I generally won't make decisions on a sample smaller than 100—and that includes demographic subsets as well. If you have 17 millennials in your 100-person sample, you won't be making any grand declarations about your millennial audience. I have a very simple rule here: if a given sample is less than 100, don't express your results as a percentage; 68 percent of 72 people is a horror movie, not a statistic.

What do I do with the results?

When you get your responses back, you may very likely be disappointed at the response rate. Face it—we are all busy, and your listeners may not respond in the numbers you had hoped. But that doesn't mean what you have is worthless. It's always best to think of a survey not as a thing to tell you what to do—you have your art, your vision, and your own road map for that. Instead, even with a small sample size, research like this can tell you what *not* to do. Survey data can give you the guardrails—the constraints that allow you to veer around the road without ever losing your way completely. Treat it thus and you won't go wrong. Research used correctly isn't about finding the safest path, the middle ground—that is why we have Celine Dion. It's about spotting the potholes so that you can speed up and take a few risks with your content without the fear of completely blowing up what makes the show great. What should your show do? People will have a thousand opinions. But what *shouldn't* you do? There you will find more agreement.

Also, as I mentioned in an earlier episode, one of the biggest mistakes people make after they have gone through the process of organizing a listener survey is never to mention it again. You should be talking about it constantly. Introduce a new feature? Explain that it came from listener feedback. Bring back a previous guest? It's because the listeners wanted to hear from them again. Always be reinforcing the value of listener feedback by showing your audience how you are putting their suggestions into action—both to improve engagement AND so they will be more likely to take the next survey.

A Sample Listener Survey

Okay! It's time to put your survey together, and to get you started, here is a pretty good template that you can customize with your show, its elements, and any other questions your qualitative discussions may have raised. Bullet points are multiple-choice questions, and where you see a blank is where a listener can write in their own answer. If you are curious about specific habits they might have, like whether or not they listen to a specific other podcast or watch a specific show, this is also the time to ask those kinds of questions.

Don't forget to make every question require a response (check with the platform you are using), and take note of whether a question is set to force listeners to pick only one answer (this is usually the default) or whether they can choose multiple answers. Let's dig in!

1a   Do you listen to…?

☐ Every episode of [INSERT PODCAST NAME]
☐ Almost every episode of [INSERT PODCAST NAME]
☐ Select episodes of [INSERT PODCAST NAME]

1b   On what platform do you typically listen to [PODCAST NAME]?

☐ Apple Podcasts
☐ Spotify
☐ Web browser
☐ Google Podcasts
☐ Castbox
☐ Podcast Addict
☐ Overcast
☐ YouTube
☐ Apple iTunes
☐ Pocket Casts
☐ Amazon Music

[This list will change over time—use your best judgment!]

1c Where else do you typically listen to podcasts?

☐ Apple Podcasts
☐ Spotify
☐ Web browser
☐ Google Podcasts
☐ Castbox
☐ Podcast Addict
☐ Overcast
☐ YouTube
☐ Apple iTunes
☐ Pocket Casts
☐ Amazon Music

[This list will change over time—use your best judgment!]

2 How long have you been listening to [INSERT PODCAST NAME]?

☐ Less than six months
☐ Six months to less than one year
☐ One year to less than three years
☐ Three years to less than five years
☐ Five years or more

[You can adjust the above answer codes depending on how long your show has been in production.]

3   In general, how soon do you typically listen to an episode
of [INSERT PODCAST NAME] after its release?

☐ Live [if your show does this!]
☐ The same day
☐ Within 48 hours
☐ Within a week
☐ More than a week after
☐ Not sure

4   How did you first discover [INSERT PODCAST NAME]?
[If your survey app allows you to shuffle these answer
choices for each listener, that would be a good idea.]

☐ Through a recommendation from friends or family

☐ Through a recommendation from another audio
program host

☐ Through an app that provides personalized
recommendations

☐ A mention on another podcast

☐ By searching the internet

☐ Through push notifications from a podcast app

☐ By hearing some or all of the podcast on another podcast

☐ By reading about it in an article

☐ By browsing an app you use to listen to podcasts

☐ Social media posts

☐ Through YouTube

☐ Through Facebook

☐ Through some other way. Please specify:

_____

5   Do you follow or subscribe to [INSERT PODCAST NAME]
    in order to know when new episodes are released?

    ☐ Yes
    ☐ No

6   Besides listening, how else do you interact with [INSERT
    PODCAST NAME]? Mark all that apply. [Shuffle order if you
    can, and also set your survey app to allow people to select
    multiple answers here, not just one.]

    ☐ Through the show's official social media accounts
    ☐ I follow the host(s) on their personal social media
       accounts
    ☐ I get the newsletter update by email
    ☐ Via Facebook
    ☐ Via YouTube
    ☐ Attend events
    ☐ None of the above

    [Note: Add or subtract answers depending on how listeners
    can interact with the show.]

7   Which of the following do you ever do while listening to [INSERT PODCAST NAME]? Mark all that apply. [Shuffle if you can.]

☐ Spending time with family or friends
☐ Cooking or baking
☐ Getting ready for bed
☐ Exercising
☐ Doing housework or chores
☐ Gardening
☐ Getting ready for the day
☐ Eating
☐ Doing crafts and hobbies
☐ Traveling for business or pleasure
☐ Not doing anything else, just listening

8   Besides [INSERT PODCAST NAME], approximately how many podcasts do you subscribe to or follow?

_____

_____

_____

9   What is your favorite podcast?

_____

_____

_____

_____

10 What other podcasts do you listen to regularly?

_____

_____

_____

_____

_____

_____

_____

11 Which of the following podcasts do you ever listen to?
    Mark all that apply. [Shuffle, if you can.]

_____

_____

_____

_____

_____

_____

_____

[Here is where you can list some podcasts that you think
your listeners might also listen to—it's helpful not only to
understand them but to identify potential shows to cross-
promote with!]

12 Have you ever told a friend about [INSERT PODCAST NAME]?

☐ Yes
☐ No

13 How would you describe [INSERT PODCAST NAME] to a friend?

_____

_____

_____

_____

14 If this podcast were to stop being made, what would you miss the most about it?

_____

_____

_____

15 Is there anything else you would like to mention about [INSERT PODCAST NAME]? For example: things you enjoy, don't enjoy, where we can improve

_____

_____

_____

_____

[This is the place to put any other questions that arose from your interviews: favorite segments, hosts, guests, etc. Try to make these multiple-choice questions as much as possible, since we are asking your listeners to write a fair amount in questions 8 to 15.

All the remaining questions are behavioral or demographic. While this information can be valuable when approaching advertisers, you do NOT need it to analyze the results of the survey. I like to put these at the end. I have left off things like education and income—these are intrusive and I don't think help you make a better show. I would, however, at least get a sense of age and gender, which will help you in the next episode]

How old are you?

_____

☐ Prefer not to answer

With which gender do you identify?

☐ Male
☐ Female
☐ Non-Binary
☐ Other:

_____

☐ Prefer not to answer

Which of the following best describes you?
Please select one answer.

- ☐ Asian or Pacific Islander
- ☐ Black or African American
- ☐ Hispanic or Latino
- ☐ Native American or Alaskan Native
- ☐ White or Caucasian
- ☐ Multiracial or Biracial
- ☐ A race/ethnicity not listed here:

_____

Episode Five
Who Are You For?

Stop Reading *Adweek*

So, you've had some in-depth conversations with some listeners about why they do or do not listen, and you've used a survey to find out how many people share the same reasons, and what else those people might have in common. It's time to start filling some buckets.

No, we haven't sprung a leak—we are going to take all this data and start building one or more profiles for the type of person who listens to your show, and that is going to help you not only find more of those people but make a better show for those people. In fact, once you have a clear visual image of exactly who your likely audience is, you can't help but make a better podcast for them. It will get into your bones—believe me, I have seen it over and over at every level of the audio business, from the smallest indie podcast to the biggest national radio show.

What you are trying to do here is to bucket your audience into a few (and here I mean one, two, or possibly three at the most) types of listener, based around their reasons for liking the show. The grist for this mill will come from questions like "How would you describe the show to a friend?" and "What would you miss if the show went away?" As you start to make sense of the answers, you will see that eventually they can all be reduced to a handful of variables. Start with the terms or concepts that sparked the most agreement around reasons someone might listen or not listen to your show—that's our first bucket, and the basis for your very first listener profile.

For instance, I once did a podcast with my wife, Tamsen, called *The Freenoter*, which was for marketing and sales executives who wanted to learn more about building their businesses through speaking, which is a big part of how we both built our respective careers. Unlike paid keynote speaking (for which there are multitudes of resources), there weren't many resources available for the "freenoter," those of us who toiled in the trenches, speaking for free in breakout sessions at conferences all over the world in hopes of attracting customers, not speaking fees.

Now, one could imagine hypothetical audience buckets for this show that fall into interest in the topic. If I were pitching it to a sponsor, I am sure I would want to talk about the high percentage of vp-and-up-level executives who listened to it. But here's what else I knew: many people listened to the show simply to hear how Tom and Tamsen, husband and wife, managed to work together without killing each other, and in fact seemingly had a blast doing it. The feedback I got from that show was as much about "relationship goals" as it was about speaking and marketing. If enough people share this sentiment, that's an audience profile waiting to be made. If most people share that sentiment, that's an opportunity to talk about a lot more than just speaking to build a business; it opens up a whole new area of topics to give the *Freenoter* treatment to, because the draw is how we manage to partner in business and in life, not specifically "speaking."

When you have isolated a group of listeners like this (let's call them a segment from now on), you can group them all together and look at the other data points they share. Are they of similar ages? Do they have similar tastes? Do they have platforms in common, or listen to your show while doing similar activities? What else do they watch, read, or listen to? If you start to see other things in common, even roughly, from a distance, then you are on the road to being able to visualize at least this segment of your audience with a lot more clarity.

As you look through all your other survey data, you might find in the leftover survey respondents one or maybe two more such buckets. Don't try to force them all together, though; sometimes there just isn't a pattern. But if you do see one or two other patterns emerge, go ahead and flesh those out as well. How are they the same as the main profile you developed? How are they different? Would they get along if they were at the same table at Applebee's, or would we have to separate them? At the very least, amongst all the incompatibilities, they have one thing in common: they listen to your show. In the same way the collectors, nine-year-olds, and bronies from the My Little Pony example have at least a plastic horse in common, your listeners always share some common ground.

At the start, though, it is going to be cleaner and easier for you to focus on one listener profile if the humans who make up that profile seem to have things in common and represent a noticeable percentage of the total survey responses you looked at. I'm going to give you some detailed examples of what these profiles look like in the next episode, but the goal of this process is to come up with a crystal clear picture and description of *who you are for*.

"Who you are for" is a very deliberate choice of words. It's more than just saying "my target audience." That's an intention, but not a decision. This choice of words says both that "my podcast would be appealing to this type of person" and "I am FOR this person"—you will ride or die for these people. You are their advocate, and everything you do on your podcast should be for their benefit and their delight. Never again will you say, "My podcast is for adults aged twenty-five to fifty-four." That's how brand marketers and people who read *Adweek* talk. A podcast that appeals to "adults 25–54" might be a trailing variable of the choices that show makes, but nobody is "for" adults 25–54. I mean, there are some bad people included in that group.

Similarly, we are going to throw out things like "I am for sports fans." That just isn't specific enough. It isn't special. There are tens of thousands of podcasts for sports fans. With very few exceptions, they are all scuffling for listeners because sports fans and even NBA fans and even

Celtics fans are all descriptors based on just one data point—this one team or topic they like—and that is all. It's based on a *what* and not on a *why*. It's like getting a spam email from someone on LinkedIn who scanned your profile and greets you with "I see you live in Boston! Here is a thing I know about Bostonians—they are looking to save money on customer relationship management software!" You forgot not to do that, champ.

Above all else, people want to be *seen*. The more specific you can get with an audience segment—the more related data points you can bring in—the more you will see these listeners for who they are beyond just "audience," and the more you can make them feel special.

Grilling with Mom

Let me give you a couple of examples of the kind of specificity in thinking we are seeking when we decide who we are for—one from the world of consumer goods, the other from entertainment media.

In an age where our pocket-sized supercomputers allow us to consume media around the clock, it's easy to forget that we don't actually have more hours in the day. As a result, certain forms of "media" have been on the decline—namely, physical word of mouth. As we spend more time with our faces buried in screens, we have less time for face-to-face social interactions.

Kingsford Charcoal noticed this trend when it saw a decrease in its sales. Fewer social gatherings meant fewer barbecues, which in turn meant less demand for its product. To counter this downward trend, Kingsford commissioned a series of market research studies to better understand the motivations and desires of its customer base.

The result of all this research was to identify a key segment they called "Everyday Grillers," and to then dig into what else these people had in common besides frequent barbecues. They used ethnographic research (actually observing people use their grill), shop-alongs, and extensive copy testing to figure out what made the Everyday Grillers tick and why they grilled so much.

The result was a much more fully fleshed-out profile of a substantial segment of Everyday Grillers who over-indexed as Hispanic/Latino, were accustomed to having large gatherings, and viewed the grill as a catalyst for getting closer together with family and friends. Kingsford pivoted its entire strategy, not around the product (it's compressed carbon, duh) but around encouraging, fostering, and providing resources for *social gatherings*. The messaging wasn't about the product; it was about reminding us that barbecues bring people together, a truth that many of us have gotten out of practice with. Remember when charcoal ads used to talk about how fast the briquettes would light?

The results were impressive: the campaign led to a 5 percent growth in dollar sales, surpassing the initial goal of 2 percent. The insights gleaned from Kingsford's research informed a comprehensive media campaign that encompassed social media and employed time- and weather-based messaging. Their success was so noteworthy that they won a Gold Prize in the Advertising Research Foundation's David Ogilvy Awards, which celebrates the use of research in advertising.

Similarly, when I was conducting the music research for Top 40 giant z100 in New York, the "ratings goal" might have been women 18–34, but that is not a cohesive group. The station wasn't going to appeal to your goth daughter who listens to Joy Division, and it wasn't going to appeal to a young professional woman who listens to country on her commute. The real profile of the ideal listener—who the station was *for*—was a very well-defined dichotomy we called "the mother-daughter coalition."

The station was put together, both in content and in messaging, to be the radio station that teens and tweens wanted to listen to in the car when their mom was driving them to school. The goal was to make a product that the younger listeners would be passionate enough about to make Mom change the station when they got in the car, but to also be the station Mom left on after the daughter was dropped off at school or soccer practice. That's not every teenaged girl, young adult woman, or young mom—and it also isn't meant to categorically exclude Dad, but that's how you start to develop a specific point of view.

Remember, just like the Joe Rogan show, you can also define your show by who you are *not* for, and sometimes that can be even more powerful. People like to feel they are part of a special velvet rope community that isn't open to everyone. Very few people want to belong to a club that includes *everyone*.

I Hope You Feel Better

One of the key things to consider about your audience, as you think about questions to ask them and what kind of information to include in a detailed listener profile, goes beyond the topic or genre of your podcast. It goes deeper than that, to how your audience *wants to feel*.

I listen to some podcasts with pretty snarky hosts. I happen to dig that, but it's not for everyone. It's easy to be snarky—it can often be my default reaction to things. Maybe that is true for you as well. But snarky doesn't age well. Sometimes, you just get sick of snark—it can be the air that you breathe if you let it. Often, a change of scenery can help. In fact, I once picked myself up out of the slough of despond with a trip to, of all places, Newcastle upon Tyne, England. I've spent a lot of time in the UK—I lived in London for a while (where I lost a million pounds, remember?) and have worked in most of the major markets throughout England, Scotland, and Wales. I love Manchester and its music, as much a product of the land as the chalk from Dover. But of all the places I've been throughout the Scepter'd Isle, none holds the unique place in my heart that Newcastle does.

I spent some time in Newcastle in the late '90s doing music research for the launch of a new radio station, which would be called Galaxy North East. Galaxy was a *fantastic* brand: positive, upbeat, and the home of dance music during the era that birthed the "Superstar DJ." It was the place to hear Darude, Basement Jaxx, or Armand van Helden. And it sounded *great* in Newcastle. In the process of doing the format research for the new station, though, the most startling insight about the market was not how well Paul van Dyk tested. It was about the *people*. This wasn't London. This wasn't Manchester. Newcastle was a different dog. The target demographic for the station wasn't listening to the Verve or Oasis or the morbid humor of Manchester's Smiths, the soundtrack to my college years. They wanted to dance, get out, and have a laugh. I was *nearly unable to process* how relentlessly positive the people I talked to were compared with the Londoners I'd had more experience with.

When the project was done, I canceled my flight home and stayed a couple of extra days at the Malmaison Hotel there, overlooking the Tyne River. Whatever they were drinking, I wanted some of that. The station reflected it. *People wanted to feel good.* It spun me around a bit. I had come to Newcastle at the end of a long batch of international projects, tired and cynical. But Newcastle was lovely because the people were actually lovely—and the station had to reflect that, genuinely, if it was going to succeed. It couldn't be wry or jaded. The music *and* the DJs had to reflect that positivity back to the city. And that is exactly what it did.

I was reminded of all that this week, when my friend Sean Ross wrote about the twenty-fifth anniversary of WKTU in New York. WKTU was launched at a time in the mid-'90s when New York City was coming out of a lull. The previous decade had seen the Big Apple go through some very turbulent times, and the music reflected that to some extent. The Top 40/pop station in town (Z100) was playing a lot of alt-rock and grunge, bands like Live, Pearl Jam, Green Day, and Sponge (???). Yes, this was "pop" in 1995. Sean can wax more intelligently about this than I, but I would just sum it up as a little dark for a Top 40 station. It reflected the times, maybe.

WKTU was the station girls would put on and listen to with their mothers in the car, and the station the boys would listen to because they wanted to be with the girls. It was the station that would reliably play and own, as then program director Frankie Blue taught me, the Song of the Summer, which we've already talked about. The morning show was RuPaul and Michelle Visage, currently the stars of *Drag Race*. The station *was* RuPaul. Genuine, upbeat, and never, ever cynical. It made you feel good and shone a beacon forward to where New York wanted to be, not where it was.

Regardless of your tone, style, or topic, ultimately you want to make your audience feel good. Maybe that takes the shape of feeling warmly welcomed or energized by the show. Maybe it is making your audience feel smugly self-satisfied and smarter than non-listeners. However that feeling manifests itself, I can guarantee you no one wants to feel bad after listening to your podcast.

This may sound blindingly obvious, but I want you to imagine being at a party—not the kind of party you would go to with your friends, but the kind that your ideal listener might go to. You are on their turf, not the other way around. What would the party look like? How would you speak to them at this party? How would you act as a *guest* of your listener?

This is in fact what you are every time someone presses Play on your podcast—you are a guest in their home. If you speak to them with contempt, or forget to take off your shoes, or don't offer to put your coffee cup in the dishwasher, you might not get invited back. Every time you press Record, you need to remind yourself that the people you are talking to are wonderful people—smart, capable, kind, and good. You are delighted to speak to them. You are mindful of their surroundings. And you aren't there to have fun at their expense. This can take many forms, as I said, depending on your tone and style. But it must never take the form of snark.

There is one thing I want to make very clear about visualizing who you are for: We aren't building a positioning statement or marketing copy. We are creating an avatar of the show's North Star that is meant *only* for you. At the end of this book, I'll give you a framework for how to talk about your podcast to the outside world. This isn't it. In fact, I wouldn't share your listener profile or persona work with anyone who doesn't work on your show. This is your scrapbook—a source of inspiration. If you nail this, your ideal listener will love your show, but there will also be concentric circles of audience around your podcast that like your show too, even if they aren't your core listeners. Being publicly specific about your "target" (I do try to avoid that word) needlessly excludes potential listeners. Why take the risk?

What I would encourage you to do, as you get more and more specific about who you are for, is to actually create a collage of pictures representing your listener. Get creative!

Give them a name, a job, a fashion sense, etc. One of the questions I used to ask listeners in focus groups about a show or a program was to imagine it was a car: What kind of car would it be? What would it look like? Who would drive this kind of car? A variation of this is to ask what kind of animal your show would be, or something equally silly (but relatable).

These kinds of questions might sound goofy, but they are time-tested ways to get people to talk articulately about things they don't normally discuss or have the vocabulary to describe. As I mentioned earlier, people can get very descriptive and persnickety when they are criticizing something but often can't find language as precise to praise. Questions about cars and animals get people out of the burden of having to be articulate audio critics and help them tap into how a show or podcast makes them feel, which is what you want.

Later, when you think about marketing and promoting your show, this collage—pictures, names, cars, and any other associated detail you can fill in—can help you find more people who fit the profile of your ideal listener. For now, though, I want you to plant the image of this listener right in front of you when you record your show. The best way I know of to make your show engaging to an audience is to *make a show for that one person and speak directly to them every time you turn on the microphone.*

You have already done the work to learn that this single avatar represents many more listeners, so you aren't really taking a risk here. If you determine that you are for retired singles who are looking to create a new chapter in their life, name her Jennifer, give her a hometown and some hobbies, and do the show for *her*. The rest will take care of itself.

As I write this, the power of AI-driven image generation is becoming absolutely uncanny, with tools like Midjourney or DALL·E 2 able to create evocative images from text prompts. It might be fun to feed all the keywords you can think of relating to your ideal listener into one of these tools, and even an image style that fits the mood of the show, just to see what our robot overlords come up with. You might get something incredibly relevant and useful, or you might get someone with eight fingers unhinging their jaw to eat a hamburger. But it might save you some time hunting the web for the exact picture you are looking for.

By the way, the advice here (to literally keep imagery of your ideal audience in front of you) applies to your co-hosts as well, if you have them. Either you all row in the same direction or you aren't going to achieve the full potential of your show. Now, you can't ask the same of your guests if you have an interview podcast, but with every question, comment, and follow-up with that guest, you should be relentless in asking yourself, What would Jennifer ask? What would she already know? What beliefs might she have that aren't serving her, and what is the best way to communicate those to her? This is the real discipline of being a host—acting as the direct agent of who you are for, not as an all-knowing narrator.

For what it's worth, I think Alex Blumberg, the former host of *StartUp* and one of the founders of the since-acquired Gimlet, is one of the best at this. He approaches every interview not as a very knowledgeable person with his own thoughts and opinions about the subject, but as a true avatar for the audience—never afraid to ask basic questions or even to appear less intelligent, all in the service of making the subject understandable and the guest relatable. "He's so smart" is not the best thing you can say about Blumberg. "He makes me think" is.

Okay, time to make YOU think. Let's put all this into practice and take a look at a couple of real-life examples of this process at work, before we return in the second half to rebuild your podcast into a lean, mean audience-pleasing machine.

Mid-roll
Putting It All Together

Case Study—The Cycle in Action

One of my audience research clients back in my Edison Research days was a well-regarded classical music station in a major US market. The station had a lot of listeners, but their average age was well into retirement. The station wanted to retain those listeners, but also find ways to expand the reach of classical music to its full potential in that city—and beyond, since the station had a very active online presence.

In podcasting, we get a lot of advice about "getting your show in front of people"—but that just doesn't work if you don't actually understand the people you are trying to get in front of. So, just as we have done in this book, I started with some qualitative research. In this case, it was a few focus groups, but again, you can do this sort of work for free with email or a Discord server. We aren't looking for answers yet. We are looking for theories.

For this project, I started with people who already listened to the station, in all age ranges, to find out some of their reasons for listening to classical music—their "whys." I think I spoke to a couple of dozen listeners over a few sessions, and gradually, three reasons for listening to classical music emerged:

* Classical music is an important part of our culture.

* I grew up playing an instrument in school and have always listened to classical.

* Classical music helps me relax.

What was fascinating to me was that few people named more than one of these reasons—there seemed to be some very clear dividing lines! There were, of course, some other reasons for listening, but these three themes seemed important enough to take to the next phase—the "who" phase—with some quantitative research.

I fielded a broad study across the whole market for anyone who had at least some positive regard for classical music, whether they listened to the station or not, to see if these themes actually held up, who these current and potential listeners might be, and how to reach them. As it turned out, all three segments were present in numbers, and they held together in some very interesting ways.

We ended up clearly defining three segments for the potential audience. All were fans of classical, but for different reasons—and those three segments were clearly different from each other.

The "Preservationists" These fans tended to be quite a bit older (seventy-plus) and were ardent supporters of the arts. They believed that classical music was an important part of the Western canon and must be supported for the good of society. As you may have guessed, this wasn't the most diverse segment, but it was a crucial one in terms of support for the station, which depended partially on listener donations. Interestingly, they didn't actually listen to the station all *that* much; classical music seemed to be more important to them as an ideal than as an actively consumed format.

The "Aficionados" This segment was largely male and late-middle-aged. Many of them had played an instrument as young students, and even though most of them no longer called themselves musicians, they had an appreciation for classical music that originated from their youth, which is uncommon. These were the kind of people who knew the composers AND the conductors, who bought classical music CDs and digital files, and who were even conversant about individual musicians and soloists.

The "Relaxers" This was the most fascinating segment to me. They tended to be female and younger than the other two segments. They didn't profess to know all that much about classical music—most couldn't tell you the name or composer of anything save the most iconic classical pieces. Instead, they turned to classical passively, as a means to work with less stress or simply to relax. They were not going to be fans of challenging, modern pieces, but used the calmer works almost as a mood service to lower their stress.

They also tended to be moms of school-aged children (which perhaps explains some of the stress) and—here was the really interesting part—did not discover classical music until later in life. Most people don't pick up an entirely new genre of music in their forties; these are typically years when people gravitate back to the songs that were popular when they were in high school. To have a segment in this age group that were actively enjoying a heretofore unknown music genre was uncommon indeed.

AS YOU CAN SEE, these three segments were fairly different, yet they all enjoyed classical music, and none of them were "wrong" for the station. I always think of them when a podcaster tells me, "I know my audience." Audiences, as we have seen, are not monolithic. They come and go for different reasons, and they are never wrong.

With a sharper view of these three segments, the station had the opportunity over time to sharpen its understanding of them, with the Cycle of Insight—using qualitative to ask the "why" questions and quantitative to flesh out the "who." In this case, we were able to go back to data from the focus groups and survey to learn more about these three segments and how to reach them.

For the Preservationists, we didn't need to do much to the product. They were more likely to be supporters of events, operas, and concerts, so the station had a marketing opportunity to bring those events to town and be visible at them. In the case of the Relaxers, we paid attention to the time of day they tended to gravitate to the station and made sure the music was a bit less cacophonous during those hours. And, as many of them were moms, we saw an opportunity to reach into school music programs with resources, especially with so many programs being cut. And we made sure there were programs for the Aficionados, especially in the evenings, when only active classical fans would be listening to the radio. The music would delve a little deeper, and the DJs would spend more time talking about the performers and the compositions.

Now, doesn't all that seem smarter than "run Face-book ads and do feed drops"? The great advantage of doing the work to understand your audience is not only that you can then optimize the product—your show itself—but also that you get a lot smarter about where else to find potential listeners online or offline. You'll also never lack for content ideas, since the diversity of an audience, tied together by at least some aspect of the show, will suggest new areas in which to cross-pollinate your podcast for years to come.

When you look at your audience through this kind of lens, you look at your podcast in a completely different way. You are able to really think like a network program-mer—weaving different segments of your audience together to keep them all engaged over time. You will begin to see them in your mind as you are talking, and you'll learn the discipline and craft of never going too long in your show before paying off each segment with something they are going to love. If you maintain this balancing act, each segment will come along for the ride and stay with you through some aspect of your show that isn't their favorite, because you have trained them to understand that they won't have long to wait before you get to that topic or feature they really love.

I talked about this in Charles Duhigg's book *The Power of Habit*, when he interviewed me about programming music and balancing familiar favorites with completely unknown music. There is nothing more dangerous on a radio station than a brand-new, unfamiliar record. But if it is bookended by huge hits, people will come along for the ride until they learn the new song and it too becomes a favorite. That's also why "Life Advice," the non-sports content on the otherwise sports-focused Ryen Russillo show, comes *last*, not first. Skillfully weaving content that appeals to the diversity of your audience will not only keep them engaged but give you more license to take risks—and that is the real competitive advantage of audience research.

Kylie Unlikely

Part of the success of the process I employed with that classical station was down to the amount of time we spent learning about the non-radio-listening lives of classical music fans; I've used the phrase "who they are when they are at home" several times to describe that work. Well, here is a little more clarity on what I mean by that, and how it can not only make your show better but also increase your revenue opportunities.

Back when we started Puremix, I conducted what was at the time the largest study to date in the UK on music tastes and how they correlated with lifestyles and even purchase behavior. We used the information about what songs people liked, what products they purchased, and what activities they enjoyed to build a detailed avatar for the audience of each station we designed.

When you go beyond simply asking questions about your show and venture into discovering more about your listeners' other interests, you gain a richer understanding of how your show fits into their lives, and this will inform your content every time you open the mic to speak. When you do this, you learn that segments of your audience often have a lot more in common than you think, which gives you other hooks and angles in your content to keep them engaged.

For Puremix, three of the stations we designed could all have been labeled as some kind of classic rock. There were clear differences in music taste, but also in income, purchase behavior, and lifestyle, that made these stations distinct from each other, and we created fully detailed ideal listeners for each. One stream, which heavily featured classic British rock from the Stones, Led Zeppelin, and the Who, we called "Pass the Lager." There was a Grateful Dead/Dave Matthews Band stream that earned the moniker "Pass the Joint," while a station that heavily featured the Police, REM, and the Talking Heads was christened "Pass the Chardonnay."

For each station, we devised a portrait of the ideal listener and made sure those details were always in front of the people doing the programming. We also supplied those personas to our sales team, so they could better target potential advertisers. (Sadly, since we launched during the "dot bomb" crash of 1999–2000, those advertisers were a little more skittish than we had hoped.)

My proudest moment was creating a persona for one of our dance stations. This station featured some new music but was heavily reliant on club classics from the previous decade. Not *too* old, but definitely not what was currently hot in the clubs of London. The listener persona for the station, based on our audience research, was a young professional woman, probably in her late twenties or early thirties, who was far enough out of school to be fully into her career but not so far as to stop going out to the clubs every now and then. So the station had to play enough music to make her "feel" up-to-date, but still have enough of the club music that was big when she was in school to bring back memories of when she used to go out more often.

In short, it was a station designed to make this fully detailed person *happy*—delighted, even. I named this ideal listener "Kylie Unlikely" and even found magazine pictures of who we thought she was.

I cannot recommend this exercise highly enough. As you flesh out who your audience is when they are at home, these details add up to create a singular listener—one person—and you can name them, list their interests, and even put together images that suggest who they are. Keep this collage in front of you when you record your show. No, really. Some of the best programmers I know do this. Ask yourself every time you open the mic if Kylie would *love* this—and if not, why are you doing it?

Okay! It's almost time to put it all back together again and turn your podcast into a *show*. But before we launch into the back half of this book, it's worth issuing a brief caveat about everything you have learned so far.

When NOT to Listen to Your Audience

Let's put our podcast aside for a moment and open a restaurant.

In fact, let's inherit one from our parents. We'll call it a diner. Our diner serves a wide variety of dishes, from pizza to burgers to salads to sandwiches. Comfort food. On any given night, there is something for everyone, and our diner becomes known for its variety. In fact, our parents really leaned into that variety, continually expanding the menu until it ranged somewhere between Cheesecake Factory and Manhattan phone book. You see these types of diners in New Jersey—they always have a sign that says *Baking done on premises*.

The diner is profitable, and there are long waits for tables on weekends—even at brunch. The town starts to grow around the diner. A Jiffy Lube pops up across the street. The strip mall next to us—you know, the one with the Blockbuster/laundromat/tax prep business—renovates. A frozen yogurt shop moves in. More people start eating out, and the guy across the street with the car wash takes notice. He demolishes that car wash, and one day— BOOM. Where once was a rack full of non-tree-smelling and yet tree-shaped air fresheners, there it stands: a new Blaze Pizza.

Now, Blaze doesn't make the best pizza you've ever had. The crust isn't going to win any awards (especially that cauliflower crust, which is neither). But the process is fun, the ability to customize your own pie is new, and the pizza is pretty good. Your friends and neighbors decide to try it with their families. Their teens and tweens love it. Next weekend, those parents return to the diner. Their teen sons and daughters ask if they can meet their friends at Blaze instead. And on Friday night, your diner is busy, because more people are eating out these days, but the character of your sales is different. Compared with previous weekend nights, you sold a lot more Baja chicken salads and hamburgers than normal, and not as much pizza. Still, it was a great night. You sleep the sleep of champions.

A year later, and the nearby disused stand-alone TV and appliance repair shop becomes a Smashburger. It's not how you would make a burger, maybe, but you gotta admit—they are tasty. By the end of the year, your most popular dish by far becomes the Baja chicken salad. You even put a star next to its name on the menu: "Chef's Favorite!" They are flying out the door. Pizzas and burgers, however, aren't selling as well. You leave the burger on the menu (and even add one—the STOMPBURGER) but decide to stop offering pizza, because pizza sales are so low that it hardly seems worth the time and effort to make the dough rise.

The next year, while it seems as if the town around you is booming, you finally notice your sales dipping. Your once-voluminous menu has slimmed to one page, front and back. On page one, smack-dab in the middle of the page in a callout box, the Baja chicken salad is highlighted as "famous." No one seems to like pizza and burgers anymore.

As business dwindles, you start to ask customers a simple question: What would you like to see more of on the menu? The waitstaff ask every customer, and after a month you collect the data, and the answer is clear: MORE SALADS. YES! You realize that based on the success of your famous Baja chicken salad, your customer base wants more salad types. Your once-vaunted variety is gone, but now you are ready to soar with your strengths with a new salad-heavy menu guaranteed to please your increasingly older and health-conscious customer base.

A year later, someone puts up a Sweetgreen, and you lose the salad business and your lease.

Here is what you missed: people used to come to your diner for variety, not salads. The salads were simply what survived because you waited to get feedback until after you lost the burger and pizza crowd. A Sweetgreen would have taken them from you, one way or another, because you were deceived by your only data source—the tastes of your ever-dwindling supply of customers. They didn't *love* your salads. They simply didn't love pizza and burgers.

Who doesn't love pizza and burgers?

There is nothing wrong with asking your current audience what they want to hear. You don't succeed in any business without super-serving your customers. But what do you do with those comment cards if your audience is actively *shrinking*? If you are reading those comment cards, you are diligently super-serving your listeners, AND your downloads are decreasing, congratulations—you have fallen into what I call *the optimization trap*.

The optimization trap is sinister. It is especially prevalent in marketing technology, with its widespread use of A/B testing. When our diner above asked its customers what they wanted more of, they said salads, but not because salads were hot. They said salads because we had already over-optimized the restaurant to serve the people who remained loyal, and we were not seeking the opinions of the customers we *used* to have, now happily munching burgers and pizzas across the street. The optimization trap is the great explanation for why Net Promoter Scores can be high and sales can be declining. You are making fewer and fewer people happier and happier.

The optimization trap affects all audience-driven media. You see it on Spotify, when Ed Sheeran puts out a new album and every track goes to the Spotify Global Top 50. You see it on the *Billboard* chart when the album by Future that debuted at number one is finally booted out of the top spot—by Future's next album, also debuting at number one.

The relentless optimization that data-driven marketing has given us has also rendered us less curious about the people who aren't giving us data. Even when your audience is growing, knowing the tastes of the people who aren't listening to you is crucial, because at some point your audience either pauses or stops growing, and you face a choice: Do I double down on what my existing audience wants, or do I test the tolerance of my current audience—AND people who aren't listening—for something different on the menu?

The answer here is that you need to widen your lens. What can you learn from the audience research you have done that can apply to researching people who aren't currently listening? There are all kinds of ways to get non-listeners to take surveys similar to the listener survey outlined in Episode Four. Some of them cost money and are accessible through some of the paid survey platforms out there, but others simply require a little creativity and sweat equity. I am a big fan of reaching listeners—and potential listeners—offline, in the real world. Where do like-minded people collect? What are some events they might go to or venues they might frequent? Could you hand out postcards at those events asking people to take a survey in exchange for some kind of contest prize, or another benefit that might be meaningful to that audience? I bet you can come up with something.

The Baja chicken salad problem is certainly real, and when you see your listenership start to decline (and not just plateau) steadily, that is a good sign that you need to get some input from the outside world into your podcast, before you end up being the absolute favorite podcast for just one person.

Okay, podcasters. Let's tack up those photos of who you are for, memorize their name, and burn every detail about them into your brain. It's time to put your show back together.

Episode Six
We Can Rebuild It

_____

Meet the Neighbors

I want to pitch a show to you. It's a show about a stand-up comic living in New York City and his everyday life. There isn't really a plot to the show; it's more about his day-to-day life and relationships with women, his career, but mostly his zany friends: an ex-girlfriend, a curmudgeonly loser, and a crazy upstairs neighbor who barges in unannounced and eats the comic's food. I'm going to call the show *Kleinfeld*.

Would you watch this show? I doubt it. What if I told you that I didn't know about that other show, this was my independent idea? You still wouldn't buy it. Whether I had done my homework or not, *Kleinfeld* is a rip-off, even if it's an unintentional one. It adds absolutely nothing new to the art.

Your podcast is an invention, and like an invention that you try to get a patent on, you have to acknowledge *the prior art*. If your invention builds on someone else's, you have to acknowledge that. And if your invention doesn't add anything new to what has already been invented, your application will be perfunctorily rejected. The creator has an obligation to be familiar with similar work and to offer something new.

This knowledge makes me ache inside when a podcaster asks me for advice about growing their show, and they tell me their show is Two Regular Fans Talking about the Cubs. This isn't a show. This is a cry for help. There are a hundred shows that feature Regular Guys Talking about the Cubs, and I can't stop you from doing another one if it gives you pleasure. But don't expect to earn an audience for that. If you can't offer a unique perspective on the subject, something novel in form, structure, or point of view, then cross-promotion isn't going to help you.

Here is a really basic thing that I don't see enough podcasters doing when they work on their show: take a spin through their neighborhood. No, I don't mean around the block where they live, but around their *podcast* neighborhood. This is my second book, and for both books I had to do some research for the publisher that identified what shelf my book would be found on in the bookstore, what books would be immediately next to it, and how my book was a different take that would appeal to the audiences of those other books.

Let me tell you, the worst thing you can hear as an author is when you tell your publisher your idea and they ask you, "Oh, have you read [book you haven't read that already published your exact idea]?" As a podcaster, you have to be prepared to handle a similar question. How can you claim to have a unique perspective on Cubs fandom if you haven't listened to any of the other Cubs fan podcasts? The answer is you can't.

Also, in the audience research that you either have done or soon will have done, you asked your listeners to name some of their other favorite podcasts. If you get some of the same names cropping up several times, it's probably a good idea to listen to those too, even if they are off-topic. Part of creating that vivid portrait of your ideal listener is understanding what else they like, and if a number of your listeners share the same favorites, that is an interesting thing to poke at, don't you think?

There is also a lot you can learn from the other podcasts in your category from the various podcast directories out there. My friend Dan Misener, co-founder of Bumper (a podcast growth agency), has written a lot about this and more intelligently than I could, and has developed a number of tools to identify what podcasts in the Apple directory would be filed next to yours on the shelves—i.e., also recommended. There is enormous value in this exercise, and not just to keep you from making another *Kleinfeld*. Using other related podcasts as a kind of whetstone can help you sharpen your own distinct point of view.

So, as you think about the point of view of your show, and those of the individual hosts or participants in the show, make sure you poke around the neighborhood and actually listen to some of those other shows. It's crucial work as you move to the next step: defining roles and goals.

Roles and Goals

Almost everything I learned about putting a successful show together I learned from my dogs. Dogs are loyal and loving, but they also have expectations, and they let you hear about it if you get them into the habit of expecting a snack at noon and then you skip that snack.

For many years, I owned a succession of border collies, who were long my favorite breed (until I got a greyhound, which ruined me for other dogs). Border collies are ferociously intelligent; you have never seen a dog more able to hold its focus, solve problems, or instinctively know what you want it to do without so much as a word.

For a while, I owned two of them at the same time—an old, cagey vet and a wily rookie on the same team. One such dog is practically a tool-user. Two? They can get up to all kinds of mischief. What I learned about the breed was that *they need a job*. They aren't the kind of dog you can just walk in the morning and then give the run of the house to all day long. They need something to do, or some kind of regular mental stimulation, or else they will demonstrate many uses for your shoes other than their designed purpose.

Without something to do, the border collie is capable of wreaking havoc on your house. Turns out, the same is true of podcast hosts. There is one podcast that I listen to every now and then that regularly has five co-hosts, and I am not sure why. They don't have jobs. I can't tell them apart. I don't know why they are all there, or what any one contributes over the others. Each topic is dealt with as a succession of "Well, let's find out what you think, Host Five."

These kinds of shows absolutely lose me, and this is my business! When I have told this story before, some smart listeners commented that I still listen to the show. Yeah, I do. But I don't recommend it, and I never will while it is still a hot mess of tangled points of view and indistinguishable voices.

Like my beloved border collies, everybody on your show needs a job. The way that manifests itself in podcasting is that each participant in a podcast should have a defined role, and they should have a distinct, audience-focused goal. If there are multiple voices on your podcast all saying "I agree with Host Three" all the time, congratulations, you have a conference panel, not a show. Shows have characters, and listeners need to be able to tell those characters apart.

By the way, even the biggest shows have this problem. I once did audience research for *The Bob & Tom Show*, one of the biggest syndicated morning shows in radio and the radio home for stand-up comedy in this country. Any comic who went through Indianapolis (the home of the show) made a stop on *Bob & Tom* to do part of their set and kibitz with the hosts, Tom Griswold (still hosting as of this writing) and his partner, the now-retired Bob Kevoian. One of the main things we heard in that research, even from some of the biggest fans of the show, was that they couldn't tell them apart, especially when they would both start laughing at the guest's jokes.

Now, this might or might not have been a show-stopping problem for Bob and Tom—but they had the benefit of the nation's best comics doing their material regularly. If you don't have that going for you, it might be time to tighten things up.

The best way to do this is to imagine the different points of view your audience might hold about a topic and to be sure that someone on the show is championing or at least speaking to that point of view, so the listener feels heard and seen. It doesn't mean they actually have to hold a particular opinion, but their character—the person they are when they are a podcast host, and not shopping in the grocery store—has to represent that role for the audience.

In big radio morning shows, you often see a construct that is known inside the industry as "the dick, the dork, and the dear." (I am not recommending this for your podcast, by the way.) The formula is that there is someone who plays the "dick," or antagonist; someone else who plays the "dork," who doesn't really fit into the conventional construct of a radio host but is there to create friction; and a third person who's the "dear," who represents the heart of the show and the person most likely to be someone the listener would call a friend in real life.

If you think about a station that appeals mostly to women, but also to their husbands, it's easy to imagine how this all plays out: the dork talks about an embarrassing situation they recently encountered, the dick says something jerky about it, and the dear gives the dick their comeuppance. Sometimes the dear is there to tell the dick, "Oh, you can't say that!" which is what most of the audience will be thinking, while the dick's job is to actually say it, even though the show rallies against them. It's why Howard Stern didn't work without Robin Quivers, and why *Inside the NBA*, the TNT halftime show that features Shaquille O'Neal and Charles Barkley, doesn't work without Ernie Johnson (the "broadcaster") being there to say, "Chuck, you can't say that!" But Howard and Chuck did say that, and either you found it funny or you rallied behind the "dear" when they were put in their place.

Now, your podcast doesn't need a dick, a dork, and a dear. But everyone should have a job or they are just running around the house, chewing up shoes. If your current cast don't have clearly defined roles and goals, then you need to either figure them out, reduce the number of voices on the show, or get smarter friends, I guess. You aren't there for them. You are there for the listener.

One of my favorite stories about this came from doing focus groups in New York for the (then) morning show at z100, the Elvis and Elliot show. Elvis Duran is currently not only the morning show host for z100 but also syndicated on nearly eighty stations around the country. But before that, he was half of Elvis and Elliot, and it's not totally unfair to imagine that Elvis was the dear and Elliot served as the dick. They would actually attend these focus groups, and I got to see Elliot watching behind the one-way glass as listeners talked about what a jerk he was, and how they loved it when Elvis or one of the other hosts corrected him or otherwise took him down a peg or two.

Elliot, ever the professional, wasn't insulted. In fact, just the opposite—it was his playing that role that made the show work as well as it did, and he knew this. Whether you loved Elliot or hated him, you had a voice on the show, and you were entertained. Not every show needs a "dick" (and I think that's the last time I am going to use that word in this book), but every host needs a defined role and a point of view, or they are just cluttering things up. As the late Dai Vernon, master of sleight of hand, was fond of saying, confusion isn't magic.

One more thing about Elvis Duran. To this day, his job on the show is the most important, but not because he is the star, so to speak (though he most certainly is, and an immense talent). What makes Elvis a genius is that he is the best "traffic cop" in morning radio. The show goes through him, at all times, and he serves as a kind of on-air director. While there are certainly producers behind the scenes, when the show is live, Elvis is responsible for what is coming out of the mic, whether he is speaking or not. To watch the show being made inside the studio is a thing of wonder, with Elvis continually making gestures and other unspoken signals to cue people to talk, or stop talking, depending on how long a bit has been going or how one-sided a point of view might have gotten.

Whether you have dorks and dears or not, if you have more than one host on your show, you need a traffic cop. It's not a glamorous job, but in practice, it doesn't work to have that responsibility fall on *everyone's* shoulders. The traffic cop has to be the host that the rest of the cast trusts to keep the show on the rails, to cut segments short when they aren't paying off your ideal listener enough, and to make sure that all the multiple viewpoints of the show are paid off dynamically and efficiently. The traffic cop has to be, as it turns out, the "dick," at least to their rambling co-hosts. Sorry—I said I wasn't going to say it again, and I said it again. This time I promise for real.

Creating a Safe Space

As you put together the structure of a show and define the roles and goals of the participants, there is one more participant you need to make room for: the listener. I listen to too many podcasts that sound like a series of inside jokes, only interesting to those who were in the room; there is no room for listeners to imagine or insert themselves into the narrative. If the voices on the show are all turned inwards, towards each other, rather than facing in the same direction, towards the audience, there is no space for your listener. "You had to be there" are words you should never utter on your show, if you want to create that space.

The act of listening to a podcast is the act of creating a space; a listener often shuts out the world and devotes all or most of their attention to this thing that sits outside their life. The podcast industry often talks about the "intimacy" of listening to a podcast, but rarely is that defined or quantified. So I'll take a stab: a secret about some of the greatest podcasts and spoken word audio shows ever made is that they created a *safe space*. Going back to my example about the bronies, if you create a podcast for bronies that does not ridicule, celebrates the values of My Little Pony in a sincere way, and provides a safe space for bronies to feel community, you've done more than "make a show about My Little Pony." You've created a safe space. People tell their friends about safe spaces.

The skill of being a great podcast host isn't light-years away from the skill of a good therapist. A host creates comfort and trust, an environment that encourages sharing, and is naturally curious without being judgmental. For millions of people, the hosts of their favorite talk radio shows and podcasts are as important for the space they create as for the air they fill.

Creating that space is the exportable skill that the great ones have, no matter the subject. Once upon a time, I spent many insomniac hours of my life listening to... um... "enthusiasts" call in to Art Bell's legendary overnight paranormal show, *Coast to Coast AM*. Bell was a legend amongst conspiracy buffs and aspirational alien abductees for entertaining a mature discussion about topics that rarely get taken seriously by the media; and he courted that mystique by living in and broadcasting from a glorified trailer in Pahrump, NV, called KNYE ("The Kingdom of Nye," for Nye County, Nevada—the home of Area 51). When Bell retired, many fans thought the show would simply die, because Bell's position in that community was irreplaceable. However, his successor, George Noory, has held on to that gig for over twenty years.

How? Because he has the same exportable skill that Bell had, that Howard Stern has, and that Larry King once had when he hosted *Open Phone America* at 3 a.m.: he creates a safe space for listeners to call in and express themselves, without ridicule.

This is why NPR's *Car Talk* persists as one of the most popular podcasts in America, and why my local NPR affiliate WBUR airs *The Best of Car Talk* every Saturday even though there have been no new shows since 2012, and one of the two "Tappet Brothers" who served as the show's hosts (Tom Magliozzi) passed away in 2014. People continue to listen to ten-year-old reruns of a show about automotive problems. I say again, people continue to listen to ten-year-old reruns of a show about automotive problems. They do this for two reasons. The Magliozzi brothers were goddamn American comedic legends, and I don't say that lightly. When they retired in 2012, Doug Berman, their executive producer, compared them to Mark Twain and the Marx Brothers and maintained that people would continue to enjoy a show about car problems years after it went off the air. Doug was right.

The second reason was that Tom and Ray Magliozzi created a safe space for smart people to be... not very smart. The most educated callers would delight in replicating every squeak and rattle, revel in their automotive ineptitude, and prostrate themselves before the wisdom of Tom and Ray in ways they probably never would at their job, or in front of family. They did so because Tom and Ray made it safe to do so. Of course, they know more about cars than we do. They never lorded it over us, or made us feel stupid for imitating the "CHUNK-KA-CHUNK-KA-CHUNK" of a bad CV joint, or the screech of a slipping alternator belt.

I think podcasters have a lot to learn from paying attention to the best of these safe spaces, because the voice of the listener is often so woefully absent from podcasting. The best podcasts make me feel as though I am a welcome member of an exclusive club (even if that club has millions of listeners), and that while non-members "don't get it," *I* certainly do. Almost no one is gifted enough to continually argue with listeners and make them feel stupid and still make a show out of it.

Have you ever seen a magician make an audience volunteer look or feel stupid for not being able to follow the card or track the little red ball? There is a term for tricks like that: "sucker effects." If that sounds bad, it's because it is bad. No one succeeds long-term by being mean to people. Only one magician in history could get away with continually telling spectators they were just "too slow" to follow him, and that was Tony Slydini ("You no see, because you no watch!"). You and I aren't going to get away with it.

Instead, let's think about ways to create safe spaces for listeners. Maybe you have an idea for a show about science—but there are already thousands of science podcasts, aren't there? But a science podcast that *welcomes listeners*—creates a safe space for getting their voices and viewpoints on the show, even a place to be "wrong"? Every show would be different, because every audience is different. In Sondheim's fantastic musical *Sunday in the Park with George*, the artist who laments being unable to contribute something new to art is counseled, "Anything you do, let it come from you. Then it will be new." Replace "you" with "them" and you've got a new show. An inexhaustible gift, really.

I'll close here by mentioning the most legendary talk show in the history of sports radio: *Mike and the Mad Dog*. There is a great *30 for 30* film and podcast from ESPN about the unlikely pairing of this increasingly combustible duo, and why they made for such "can't miss" afternoon radio every day on WFAN in New York City. (I lived in NYC then, and I was *hooked.*) But what many people fail to recall is that there were really three stars on that show: Christopher "Mad Dog" Russo, Mike Francesa, and Doris from Rego Park. Doris lived with her parents until her death at age fifty-eight; she had had numerous surgeries throughout her life to deal with complications from neurofibromatosis and was in constant pain. She called in all the time to talk about her beloved Mets.

Mike and Chris berated each other all the time. But they never berated Doris. She coughed a lot. Sometimes her voice was pretty weak. Mike and the Mad Dog always made sure it was heard.

When you do the work of discovering the why of your listeners, one of the things you have to keep digging for is this: Are they looking for a safe space? And can my show offer that to them and never make them the butt of the joke? The greatest podcasts in existence do this all the time—and understanding this principle is the core of getting to the whys of your listeners.

Workshopping Your Podcast

At the beginning of this episode, I talked about how authors are required to review related books and influences if they are trying to get published by a traditional publisher, and how podcasters don't do this often enough. There is another helpful concept from the world of writing, whether it's fiction, nonfiction, screenplays, or scripts: the rough draft. I'm going to spend the entire next episode on the craft of editing your podcast, but as you think about refining your podcast, don't forget about the value of beta listeners in the process.

Some podcast consultants will tell you to just hit Publish—get it out there and learn from your mistakes. I hate making mistakes. They say you learn from your failures. Well, I've learned that I hate to fail. There's a kind of mythology about failure in entrepreneurial circles. How many of you have heard the term "fail fast"? There's a kind of common sense to this concept, I think. After all, if you have the chance of failing, you should figure out what the problem is sooner rather than later. If you can test and iterate quickly, you'll spend less time, and therefore less money, figuring out what doesn't work so that you can more rapidly get to what does work without significant sunk costs. John Krumboltz and Ryan Babineaux took the term even further and wrote a whole book called *Fail Fast, Fail Often*, which adapts this thinking to life and business choices.

It's interesting to me how this term has been co-opted by creators. "Fail fast" was originally a term used by computer programmers in a system called "agile development." In agile development, a team of programmers engages in what is called a "scrum," which is a framework for a fast, incremental approach to writing code in a short period of time, testing it to see what breaks, and then iterating quickly. It's a great way for programmers to eat the elephant one bite at a time and make measurable progress on a large coding project.

Makes sense if you are a coder, right? Dash off some code, watch it break, fix it, move on. But apply that logic to, say, running a restaurant. Okay, so pork sushi didn't really work and made a lot of people sick, but hey—at least we figured that out in the first week, right? Let's get back on the horse and get a new menu out there tomorrow.

If a piece of code fails, that coder doesn't lose their job. They go home, drink some Mountain Dew, play some *Apex Legends*, and come back the next day and fix it. That restaurateur, though? Might not be so lucky.

The influential author and speaker Seth Godin is a famous proponent of failing fast and has been quoted as saying, "The person who fails the most, wins." He is also well-known for his "Ship It" mantra, which advocates for releasing your products and ideas into the wild before they are perfect, learning from your mistakes, and iterating your way to success. In an article entitled "The Truth about Shipping," he wrote: "Ship often. Ship lousy stuff, but ship. Ship constantly. Skip meetings. Often. Skip them with impunity. Ship."

This has become a popular manifesto with start-ups, but I think it is a particularly dangerous one for podcasters. Here's what is right about it: the need to iterate. Any truly great product is the culmination of Frank Turner's "tally of mistakes and successes," an ongoing series of continual improvements. I think that's indisputable. The inventor Thomas Edison was once famously quoted as saying, "I have not failed. I've just found ten thousand ways that won't work." Noted British inventor James Dyson built 5,127 prototypes of his bagless vacuum before hitting upon the one that worked. That's a lot of failure—and certainly, if you are going to fail that much, you are going to want to fail fast!

Those two stories are often cited by entrepreneurs as the very model of failing fast and the power of iteration. But those stories are often misused, and horribly, in the service of the fables of innovation. Let me tell you one thing that neither of those two notable failures did:

Ship it.

Edison didn't ship 9,999 crappy light bulbs. Dyson didn't ship 5,000 vacuums that sucked (or didn't suck, as the case may be). They iterated. They tried. And they failed, over and over.

But not in the marketplace. Not in public.

So you see, I do believe in the power of failure. And if you are going to fail, failing fast beats failing slow six ways to Sunday. But I also know this: failing sucks. Failing in public, especially with the early adopters so crucial to advocacy, sucks even more. So I'd rather fail as little as possible, and fail behind closed doors when I can.

All of this ties back to the making of things, like a podcast, in this way: Make your crappy first podcast. Make your crappy fifth podcast. But also don't be afraid to hide it under the mattress if you aren't proud of it. It only takes one bad experience with a Dyson for you never to consider buying a Dyson again. It only takes one listen to a poor podcast to convince that listener that they don't need to listen to your stuff ever again.

But I don't want to put any more pressure on you. What you need—what we *all* need—is a place to fail, in private. So here's the tweet: *Writers' Workshops, but for Podcasters.*

When I was a graduate student in literature, I was occasionally part of some writers' workshops. Each week, we would take in snippets of what we were writing, share them with our peers, and get critical feedback. These workshops can be *humbling*. Nobody likes to be told that their baby is ugly. But the reward for enduring those brutal truths is the potential to create something better—maybe even something great. The writers' workshop is a place to fail before you ship.

I think there is a place for the writers' workshop in podcasting as well. No, this isn't a million-dollar idea. I don't have an app ready. But I think more podcasters would benefit from what writers have had for years—a safe space to preview their work in front of an audience of their peers before it is birthed to the world. For those of you creating a weekly show, maybe there are three or four other weekly podcasters you could join up with and form a common goal to make each other's episodes that week the best they can possibly be.

This only works if all the chairs face each other. This is a gathering of peers, and everyone has to play at the same level. You don't have to take everyone's advice. You *do* have to *listen* to it. It's all information. And in the often lonely and information-starved world of the podcaster (especially the solo podcaster), a podcasters workshop might just make the difference between a good show and a *great* show.

Unless you are truly producing an exclusively live show and not a podcast, there is no reason to ship something you know could be better. That doesn't mean you strive for perfection, or even close to perfection. You do, however, strive for *better*. Seeking critical input from peers during the process of retooling your show is one way to get there.

The other way? It's so important that it deserves its own episode.

Episode Seven
It's Time to Eat the Frog

Dreaditing

This may be one of the most controversial chapters in this book, but I feel I need to make a strong statement here.

If you want to grow an audience and you are not editing your podcast, you are making a big mistake.

Editing is one of those seemingly contentious topics in podcasting that ought not to be, really. Does anyone truly believe that a podcast wouldn't benefit from at least some kind of post-production polish? Surely not. Yet editing is one of those daunting topics that is a stumbling block for people, a point of procrastination—even a mental roadblock to actually publishing your show.

Look, I get it. Editing is hard. When I started in radio as a teenager, I used to have to edit my own commercial reads with reel-to-reel tape and a utility knife. And no, I am not seventy years old. You can easily spend more time editing your podcast than you do recording your podcast, and perfectionists can well and truly get lost in the process.

Here is what you *don't* need editing for:

1 Making a podcast
2 Making money with your podcast

I know loads of people who just post the show, largely untouched, and bang out podcast after podcast, week after week. And some of them even make money doing this—especially if their podcast is a lead-generation tool for another business, or if they have a great relationship with a sponsor or direct support. If editing stops you from making a podcast, then don't edit.

But that's not why you bought this book, is it? No, you bought this book because you want to grow your audience, and the only key to growing an audience is to put out impeccable work. One of my favorite quotes is by J.J. Watt, one of the greatest defensive players in NFL history. Once, when asked about his insane training schedule, he responded, "When it comes down to that moment, when it's me against you, you know in your head whether you worked hard enough. You can try to lie to yourself. You can try to tell yourself that you put in the time. But you know—and so do I." Hopefully, working on your podcast is not a violent collision with an offensive tackle, but the core message is this: putting out work that is "good enough" means that you could have done better, and you know it. And this is not who we are, dear readers. We are here to do the work.

What exactly are we editing?

Let's agree on a few things to start with. When I say "edit your podcast," there are really three things that I think anyone can learn to do without requiring a degree in audio production. All of these things do require software that allows you to select, delete, and move around audio clips, whether that software is free, like Audacity or GarageBand, or costs money, like Adobe Premiere or Hindenburg. Here are the three things:

1 Eliminate obvious mistakes
2 Make judgment calls
3 Advance the plot

Obvious mistakes

I hope I don't need to say too much about this. If you drop an f-bomb in the middle of a podcast that is NOT marked explicit, edit that fucker out. In addition, butchering names, tongue-twisters, false starts, and anything else that trips you up in the recording process needs to go, without debate. Anyone who tells you that you don't need to edit these "authentic" things out of your podcast has never attracted a significant audience—by this, I mean fifty thousand unique humans per episode or more. You show me someone who attracts that kind of audience without editing and I guarantee they have some other kind of distinct advantage, like celebrity or a fifteen-year head start. Most of the advice I see about "being authentic" with your podcast comes from people who have never achieved the lofty audience-size goals that you and I are seeking, my friend.

I think it is worth saying something here about that oft-abused term, "authenticity." Your version of authentic isn't my version of authentic, and it isn't anyone else's version either. Authentic is not a synonym for "unfiltered"; authentic is presenting yourself in a way congruent with your beliefs and values. For example, I do a lot of public speaking, and I rarely, if ever, swear onstage. Am I a prude or morally opposed to vulgarity? Five minutes with me off-stage would put the lie to that. But my mission is to grow podcasting as much as I can, and part of that is to coerce as many podcasters as I can to do better work. If I drop some f-bombs onstage, I will turn off some portion of my audience, and they will be less receptive to my message. And that is not congruent with my mission. So, the fact that my language onstage is more measured and restrained than the language I use in social settings is 100 percent congruent with who I am and how I want to be perceived. That is MY authentic. Anything else is just how someone else wants you to act, and that's about them.

Remember that.

So, back to our obvious mistakes. The vast majority of these are things you know you did the second you said them, so a great habit to get into is to loudly clap once into the microphone immediately after you screw up. This makes each edit point blatantly obvious when you are editing the show after the fact: look for the single big vertical line in the middle of your audio waveform, and that's an edit point. Easy peasy. I record a five-minute daily news podcast about the business of podcasting called *The Download*, and because it is so short, I am more likely just to restart than to clap and move on, but anything longer than five minutes and that's probably wasting your time. Just clap, redo the wonky bit, and keep going.

There is no reason to leave obvious gaffes in your podcast. You aren't Oprah. You need every advantage you can get, and it starts with flawless audio.

Judgment calls

These almost fall into the category of obvious mistakes, but they are at least debatable. I am reserving this category exclusively for long pauses, thinking noises, and filler words like "umm," "ahhh," "you know," and other crutches. Again, you will have some podcasters tell you that they never edit these out because they are "authentic," and again, I ask you to press them for their audience numbers. Other podcasters will spend hours editing them all out, so that the speech flows like the spice of Dune, unfettered by anomalies. I think the truth is closer to the latter, but not always, and here is how I would make the distinction.

In most cases, filler words and other verbal crutches are simple *disfluency*: I know the right word, it's just taking me a while to get there. Especially when you are editing an interview with someone else, and your goal is the transfer of information, why not clear that stuff up? It makes your guests look good and provides a better transfer of information. A podcast isn't meant to be live. If it is live, fine—but for the product you put "on wax," hosted as a media file for all perpetuity, or at least until you stop paying your hosting bill, why not pare away anything that interferes with the clean transfer of information? We all have vocal crutches, but you aren't a recorder of speeches. That is a non-skilled position. You are a podcaster. Make a show.

Some apparent disfluencies and hesitations, though, are meaningful. They signal an actual hesitancy to speak or a difficult topic rearing its head. In these cases, when a subject (even if that subject is you) is dealing with something beyond simple disfluency, it can be meaningful to transfer that feeling to the listener. There is a huge difference between struggling to articulate an emotion and struggling to remember the antonym for "elongated." Don't remove silence if it's meaningful—but make it rare, and make it count. Otherwise, you are just wasting your listeners' time.

Don't believe me? Take a one-hour podcast that hasn't been edited, edit out EVERY snippet of silence, hesitancy, disfluency, and filler word, and save ALL those snippets to a single separate file. Label that file "MY AWSUM PODCSAT." Now listen to THAT podcast. Yeah, I thought so.

The plot

Okay, now it is time for the real work. Everything we have discussed to this point is table stakes—there is no reason for you to put out a podcast with obvious mistakes or stretches that make you or your guests look bad. That's just effort. But here is where you turn your podcast into a show by using this great gift you have: the modern ability to edit and move around audio to tell a story with simple, accessible tools and some effort.

Most podcasts I listen to suffer from what the British would call losing the plot, which means exactly what you think it means. Now, if you are creating a scripted fiction podcast, your ability to not lose the plot is probably beyond the scope of this book and down to whether or not you are a talented fiction writer, not a podcaster. But if your podcast is not fiction, whether you script it or not, I think you'll find some value here.

I'm going to start with a bold statement: *all podcasts should be scripted*. No, really.

That doesn't mean you have to write a script and then read your podcast from that script. That clearly isn't how an interview would go, for instance. But once that interview is complete, you *do* have the opportunity to script your podcast *after the fact*, before you post the file. To me, scripting your podcast simply means making sure it adheres to a strong narrative arc and eliminates needless material. You are creating content, just like a writer; and like a writer, you can examine all the parts and pieces of your content to determine what goes where and what should stay under your bed. This is the work that few do.

There are three stages to this, and if you break the process down this way, you will find it easier than you think.

A Throat Clearing

This is a term a writing professor of mine in grad school used to use all the time; it's also the sin of which I am most guilty in my own writing. Throat clearing is any kind of non-narrative machination that happens before you get into what you are actually trying to say or ask. It often happens at the very beginning of podcasts, as the hosts kibitz with each other about where they've been that week, what they've been doing lately, or what they had for dinner. Now, I am not suggesting those elements don't belong in your podcast; people do listen to podcasts for character, and character definition is important. But do you need to start the show with it? Does a new or even new-ish listener care yet? Start with what they know—the topic they tuned in for—as an entrée to the things they don't yet know and you have a better chance of making them care.

In writing, throat clearing can happen at any moment, not just at the beginning. Any long-winded preamble can turn into this without discipline. Nine times out of ten, when a podcast host starts a story with "This requires some setup... " I find the payoff not to be worth the added narrative cruft. Maybe, when you speak the story into the mic, you might feel the need to embellish details, but challenge yourself in the editing process. How much can you pare away and still retain the meaning and impact of the narrative? If you have a co-host or other collaborator, ask them. I bet you need less than you think to get your point across.

My friend Mitch Joel, whose podcast *Six Pixels* is the longest-running business podcast I know of, generally starts his show completely cold with his guest by simply asking them, "Who are you, and what do you do?" No long bios, no throat clearing, no rambling introductions. Save that for the blog post or the show notes. If someone is listening to your show, *they are already listening to your show*. Get on with it.

B The Order of Things

Because recording a podcast is, in the moment, an often unscripted effort, things don't always come out in the best order. Sometimes a guest will remember something later that pertained to a question asked at the beginning. Dialogue can hop around, logically and temporally. Non sequiturs happen. Not every guest (or host) is always at their most coherent. Indeed, some guests simply aren't particularly fluent on a microphone, but the information they have to share is nonetheless vital and meaningful to your audience.

The solution here is to use the editing process to move the chunks of content around and craft a stronger arc. Again, this isn't as hard as it sounds if you have modern editing software that lets you highlight segments of audio and give them meaningful labels. I find it helps to give these clips a short label and then create a separate document that offers a little more clarity (or even a transcript) of each segment so it is easier to move them around.

Whenever I write a speech or give a research presentation, I do this with index cards. The order that I spit things out from my brain, or the order of questions in a research deck, is not necessarily the strongest order in which to present the information. I tend to be a visual thinker about information chunks like this, and most editing software allows you to organize your oral content in this way.

There are two helpful things to keep in mind as you do this: information dependencies and the audience's next question. If a piece of information that comes later in the show is required or even just helpful to understand better something that happened earlier in the recording, ask yourself if it would be clearer or aid in knowledge transfer if you just moved it up. Sometimes information dependencies can even be filled in after the show is recorded. For instance, you might go back and research something that the guest had a fuzzy memory of, and then insert that clarification in post-production. Why not? If it makes the job easier for the audience, it is generally worth doing.

That leads naturally to the second helpful mindset: always have the audience's likely next question in mind. If you are interviewing a raw food advocate and they tell you that they never cook any greens except for fiddleheads, it doesn't matter how compelling your next question or their answer might be—your audience isn't thinking about it. They won't be able to let go of the question in their head: Why don't you eat raw fiddleheads? Nothing you do will register until you acknowledge and answer the question in their head.

This turns out to be a great way to structure any podcast. Any construct that asks an audience to believe something different or new doesn't just start with that new belief. Instead, it's a series of "If you believe this, then you should believe that" statements, building bit by bit until a logical conclusion is reached. If you structure your show to ask and answer these little questions as they pop up in the mind of a listener, they will follow you all the way to the end.

C Remember Kylie

Earlier, I told you about my favorite listener avatar of all time, Kylie Unlikely. If you have gone through or at least thought about the processes I've described earlier in the book, you too should have some very clearly defined avatars for the precise humans you are aiming your podcast at. In the editing process, you should have a picture or collage of your own Kylie Unlikely taped to your monitor. As you are going through each snippet of content, ask yourself the following questions:

- Does Kylie understand this without context?
- Is Kylie interested in this?
- Would Kylie LOVE this?

Anytime someone opens the mic on a podcast, they should be hitting at least number one and number two. The third is a lofty goal, but if you can't create those moments at least once in a while in an episode, you aren't going to be Kylie's favorite thing, and I want you to be Kylie's favorite thing. To do that, you have to ruthlessly examine your podcast and eliminate all the things Kylie doesn't care about. This means killing some darlings, even a favorite story. If it isn't for Kylie, it's for you—and you already listen to your show, so what's the point?

By the way, I know plenty of successful radio morning show hosts and program directors who do indeed have images or collages pinned to bulletin boards to constantly remind them of who their core listener is. If you are sarcastic and snarky, but the visage of your ideal listener looking back at you is guileless and kind, you are never going to connect. Ask any failed Top 40 DJ.

Mid-roll: How long should my podcast be?

There are any number of answers to this question, which is a top-three question when people approach me at podcast conferences. There are three answers to it, in increasing order of correctness:

1   22 minutes, because that is the length of an average commute. This is a terrible answer and invalidated by the number of one-hour podcasts at the top of the charts. The very point of podcasting is convenience; it can adapt to any listening window you have. Besides, there is no such thing as a 22-minute commute. That is just the average of the people who have 90-minute commutes and the people who work at home and have no commute.

2   As long as it needs to be to tell your story, and no longer! This answer sounds better, but still offers very little guidance, and depends on YOUR perception of YOU telling YOUR story—which is not how we build an audience, is it? You know better by now.

3   And here is my answer: *shorter than your last one.*

Using a clear and ruthless editing process for your content in the way I have outlined in this chapter will naturally make your podcast shorter—I guarantee that. You might find that a show you think "has to be an hour" would be better at 25 minutes. Go with that. Remember, there is no quality vs. quantity in podcasting. There is only quality. If you are consistent and strong in removing elements that are meaningless to your intended audience, no one is going to talk about your podcast being too long or too short. This is the basis behind one of the audience survey questions from Episode Three: "Does my podcast feel too long or too short, and if so, what would you expand/cut?" Ultimately, it's not about a length of time, but how you make an audience feel. This has little to do with you telling your story.

It's Time for Surgery

Over time, you may get good enough at podcasting that you will do many of the things we have talked about in this chapter live, in the recording process. That takes a LOT of reps, and it also takes you going through a fairly painful diagnostic procedure on a regular basis—like a colonoscopy for your podcast. In fact, let's just call it your podoscopy. It's *slightly* more fun than a colonoscopy and doesn't require changes to your diet.

Your first step: get *the most detailed transcript possible*, done by a human, of a recent episode. There are lots of AI or machine-assisted transcription services, and even software like Descript that lets you edit your audio from a transcript of your show. These may be great for your editing process, but for your podoscopy, we want no mistakes—we want a painstakingly accurate transcription of every word, filler word, and noise made on the show, with detailed time codes and clearly labeled speakers. This is the kind of thing a top-tier transcription service can provide. (An AI won't get it all and won't be accurate.) You want a human to do this, and you want them to take their time.

What you are looking for costs more than a machine transcription—sometimes a lot more. While you can find many free tools to simply take a shot at this, services that provide accurate transcription, including time stamps and speaker identification, can be two to four dollars per minute, which adds up for a 60-minute podcast (yet another incentive to produce a shorter show).

The result of this process should be an absolutely verbatim account of everything that was audible on your show, who said it, and how long everything took (including silences). You should, I believe, be horrified at this. To reach that state, it doesn't take too many pages of reading "...ummm...ummm...it's like...ummm...when, you know, when you take and, when you take a whole, like, day and, like, kind of, relive your show or whatever, right?" At first, it should make you want to burn it all down. Keep that feeling! This is one of the best ways I know to teach yourself the craft.

Once you have that transcript, go through it—with your co-host(s) if you have one—and challenge everything. Circle all the easy mistakes and dead air and disfluency. You know they should have been edited out. Identify content that is out of order or lacks a logical dependency. Rewrite a segment if it makes the content better. You can't rewrite a guest, but you can make them sound better by filling in details that should have been in the first take. And, most importantly, keep that picture of Kylie handy. If it doesn't play with Kylie, cross it out.

There is nothing worse, by the way, than seeing a completely accurate transcript of yourself speaking. I have spent many, many years doing focus groups for brands, and those groups are routinely transcribed accurately by humans so that my clients and I have a record of everything that happened—a record that could be read dispassionately after the emotions of the "event" were over, to be sure we still had the same perceptions we held during the group itself. So I have REAMS of pages of me going "umm... ahhh..." and repeating myself. It's torturous to read and torturous to have to send to a client.

So why would you send that to a listener?

This is an especially good practice to do with a friend and certainly your co-host(s). Challenge everything. Why did you say this? Could you have done this shorter? Don't forget to praise, either—there are bound to be some really nice moments on your podcast. What made those moments crop up, organically or otherwise? What were the conditions that made them possible? What was your level of preparation, and how did that influence the flow of the audio?

If you are putting out a show every week or so, this is a great exercise to do once a quarter, or at least a couple of times a year. It will do two things: make you more attuned to the editing process, but also make you sharper in the moment, when you are actually recording your audio. I say this with love, and as a fellow traveler: there is a shocking amount of irrelevant content in the average podcast. If you don't clean that up before you start marketing your show, you are just inviting people to have a bad experience and never come back. But if you do engage in this process—a regular podoscopy—and let that experience filter into your editing and your actual narrative flow, you will most assuredly set yourself apart from the 99 percent who won't do this work.

That's really the best news about all this: nothing in this episode, save a quality transcription, really costs any money. It is all sweat equity. You may find that you can't do all of it in a week. What would happen if you took the time it required and published every other week? Or every other month? I'll tell you what would happen: you would be prouder of your work, and you would have a better chance of growing an audience.

We are almost ready to launch our revamped, audience-focused, leveled-up podcast! Just a few last finishing touches to add some polish, which is the focus of our next episode.

Episode Eight
Finishing Touches

_____

Music

One easy way to level up your podcast is to get more intentional with your use of sound and music. Music is a powerful tool that can instantly create an atmosphere or convey emotion. The right music can set your podcast's mood, whether it's upbeat, mysterious, melancholic, or energetic. This can prepare listeners for the content and make them more receptive.

I use some kind of music in every podcast I create, and nearly every successful show I have ever consulted on or worked with has made use of audio cues. Music plays a crucial role in podcasting, not only in setting the mood and tone but also in enhancing the overall listening experience. More than that, using music or other sound cues to call attention to regular, recurring segments in your podcast provides a bit of a mental "road map" to listeners that gets them ready for a change. It can help break up different sections of your show, signaling to listeners that the topic or focus is shifting. This can be especially useful in longer podcasts or ones with multiple segments.

For these kinds of elements, brevity is key. One of my favorite devices is a simple bell, like the kind you whack at the front desk of a hotel to get someone's attention. In *The Dan Le Batard Show*, there is a Monday segment where one of the team, Jon "Stugotz" Weiner, rattles off a rapid-fire series of weekend observations from the world of sports. Left unchecked, this segment could be fatiguing and hard to follow, but someone (maybe Stugotz himself) dings a bell between each observation to punctuate the line and even cue for laughter. Pavlov knew what he was talking about.

Sound cues also play a major role in differentiation. When thousands of podcasts sound like generic voices talking into microphones, a unique set of sound cues, intro and outro music, and transitional elements makes your podcast immediately recognizable. Your music becomes synonymous with your podcast's brand, and over time, listeners will immediately recognize your podcast just by hearing the first few seconds of your theme tune.

I'll touch on how I use music and sound in a moment, but first, here are some general tips.

How and when to use music

- **Intro:** Your podcast's opening music should capture your show's essence, creating an immediate connection with first-time listeners and a sense of familiarity with regular ones.

- **Outro:** This signals the episode's end and can be a variation of the intro music or a completely different track that provides closure.

- **Transitions:** If your podcast has different segments or switches between themes, a musical interlude can ease these transitions.

- **Background:** Gentle ambient music can be used underneath spoken content, especially during emotional or meaningful moments, to emphasize and elevate the narrative. This is not a thing to do under your entire podcast, as it can be distracting, but for a short segment with quick hits or other kinds of rapid-fire content, it can provide a useful contrast with the rest of the show.

- **Emphasis:** Music can be used to highlight particular moments, create suspense, or bring attention to a specific point.

- **Relevance to topic:** Choose music that aligns with your podcast's theme. For instance, a podcast on '80s pop culture might use synth-heavy tracks, while a horror podcast could lean into eerie, suspenseful music.

Technical considerations

- **Volume levels:** Ensure the music isn't too loud compared with the spoken content. Listeners shouldn't have to struggle to hear what's being said.

- **Quality:** Use high-quality tracks to ensure clarity and avoid distortion.

- **Duration:** Keep intros and outros concise. While they set the mood, they shouldn't be so long that they deter listeners from the main content. Ten to fifteen seconds, max. Seriously—count to fifteen sometime and tell me when you are bored.

Potential challenges

- **Copyright issues:** This is a significant concern. Always ensure you have the rights to use a track. Even if you're not monetizing your podcast, using copyrighted music without permission can lead to legal issues and having your podcast taken down from platforms. There are numerous royalty-free music libraries available, but sometimes you might want a specific track, which may require purchasing a license or paying royalties.

- **Overuse:** While music is a fantastic tool, don't overdo it. Too many musical interludes or consistently loud background music can distract from the content and annoy listeners. Music elements shouldn't overshadow your content. Opt for tracks that complement your voice and the message, rather than compete with them.

Here's the advanced class for extra credit. When I choose music, I first think about the mood I want to create, how I want the listener to feel when they first click Play. More than that, I focus very clearly on my intended listener: Would this feel familiar to them? Jarring? Think about your podcast as a room that you are welcoming your ideal listener into. What should be playing in the background to make them feel at home? When they leave, how do you want them to feel?

Often, I hear music at the beginning and end of a podcast that doesn't make any sense to me. It's generic rock music or something you might hear at the beginning of a corporate HR video on VHS. It's just "there," not doing anything. Sometimes the music I hear on podcasts isn't internally consistent—the intro and outro seem completely unrelated. Every piece of audio branding in your show should enhance its internal consistency. If you have a favorite restaurant, bar, or club, you wouldn't want it changing its theme and style every week.

What I like to do, after imagining the "room" I want to create for my listener, is go to one of the major sites for royalty-free music. (I use Pond5, but there are other good choices.) I start to search for music using descriptors for the mood I want to create, and then start auditioning tracks. Sometimes I will listen to hundreds before I find one that really works. When I do, I tend to stick with the same creator/composer and find other tracks in the same family. You will find that the best composers on a site like Pond5 create a whole suite of tracks and sounds around a particular mood or vibe, which does a lot of the work for you.

When Tamsen and I created *The Freenoter*, we wanted to evoke a 1960s cocktail lounge, so I auditioned tracks for a good four hours before finding one that felt as if I was watching an old episode of *Laugh-In*. (Ask your grandparents about that one, kids.) There was also a kind of game-show-y segment, so I sourced a jingle that sounded exactly like it came from a 1960s TV game show, to keep the mood in the same era. Every sound element on the show was designed to make listeners feel as though they were sitting in a cocktail lounge on the Strip in Las Vegas in 1968, having a martini with Frank.

For the *Sounds Profitable* podcast and its associated daily news show, *The Download*, I wanted to create a sound that would stand in stark contrast to the urgent and breathless tone of most news programs. Both podcasts tend to be calm, relaxed, and devoid of spicy-hot takes on the news, so I wanted the mood to be set early on: this was a quiet space, where the news of podcasting is discussed in a thoughtful manner. After all, as my partner Bryan often reminds me, there are no podcast emergencies.

To accomplish that, I found a very chilled-out trip-hop track and associated sound elements that immediately telegraph to the listener that this is not your typical daily news show. There's no ACTION NEWS BLAST or telegraph noise or thunderbolts—just a relaxing trip-hop beat that fades into a warm, friendly tone. (I smile when I read the news stories, which helps.)

The most important thing in all this is that music can absolutely level up your podcast if (and only if) it is internally consistent, is pitched to your ideal listener, and creates the room they would want to hang out in.

Audio Quality

Speaking of sound, here's a thing that needs to be said. If you spend any time scrolling through social media or podcast discussion boards, you will see endless variations on this theme: "Your content is the most important part of your podcast. It's more important than your mic, your recording environment, your sound design, your editing software, and if you even edit at all."

Seems like a non-threatening thing to say. In fact, as far as podcasting advice goes, it's probably the most retweetable thing on Twitter, the most threadable thing on Threads, and the most, uh, xecrable thing on X.

This often gets spun into a piece of received wisdom that tells you not to worry about these things. Just make great content. Arguing against this stance is not exactly populist rhetoric in podcasting. To quote Ben Affleck in *Boiler Room*, just before he picks up his Ferrari keys, "That's what's possible. Let me show you what's required."

It is 100 percent true that the only thing you need to make a podcast is content and the mic built into your laptop. Turn it on. Speak your piece. Make your art. Don't let your equipment stop you. Congrats, you've got a podcast.

That is not what this book is about. If you want a podcast, the recorder app on your phone is all you need. We are trying to get you an *audience*. If you want an audience, if you want a *show*, the math is a little different.

Let's take the elements of a podcast and set them to equal a hundred. How many of those points would you assign to content ONLY? Let's say, for the sake of argument, that content is 70 percent of a show. To avoid harder math, let's say sound quality and design are the other 30 percent. Sure, we can quibble about the details.

So, if you take an unedited, unprocessed, undesigned, and underthought-about podcast straight off the Air-Pods, how many of those 30 points do you think it would earn? Well, audio quality and editing are a little more pass/fail than on a spectrum, but let's be charitable and say 10 out of 30.

Now, how good is your content? No, really. Does it earn 70 out of 70? Perfect? The *Citizen Kane* of podcasts? Would you give yourself an A? How about a B? On a 70-point scale, a solid B is 59 points.

So, add that up: 10 + 59 = 69. No gibbering in the back, now. That's a failing grade. It would have been so easy to pass this test, even with middling content, if you had spent more time on the other 30.

When I was a kid, I remember HBO becoming available on cable. It wasn't digital then, as I am one of the olds. Everyone got a scrambled signal, and if you paid to subscribe, the cable company would unscramble it.

If you had the patience of a saint, four Advil, and a good imagination, you could almost kinda watch a movie on scrambled HBO. The screen would jitter and roll like a misaligned VCR, but you could hear the sound, and occasionally the jitters would slow enough for you to make out the actor.

I remember very clearly watching one entire movie this way: the HBO premiere of *Alien*. I wanted to see it SO BAD as a kid, but it was rated R, and presumably, if I watched it, I would turn out bad or something. This one is still up in the air.

So yes, I put up with a garbled picture, distorted sound, and the black-and-white cheap-ass TV I had in my bedroom, got up at midnight, and "watched" the whole thing.

You might think I am arguing against myself here. So, content *is* all you need, then?

Yes, if your podcast is *Alien*, and you are Ridley Scott.

Don't let anyone tell you that you need to edit your show or have great audio quality to make a podcast. But, equally, don't let anyone tell you that you *don't* need those things to attract an audience.

You deserve a podcast. No one deserves an audience. The 70 percent is a magical combination of talent, kismet, and celestial alignment. But the other 30 percent is a repeatable, methodical, learnable process that just takes a little more time and a few extra bucks. Why not take the easy "W" here and give yourself a little "extra credit" in a sea of middling shows?

Get the best microphone you can afford that also suits your voice. If you fancy a field trip, B&H in New York City has an entire treated microphone room where you can audition dozens of microphones to hear exactly how you sound in them. I am not going to make specific recommendations, but if you don't record in a treated studio, you are going to be better off with a dynamic microphone than its more sensitive cousin, the condenser microphone. For what it's worth, even though I record in a noisy downtown apartment, I DO use a condenser mic, but I turn the gain way down (so it doesn't pick up much extraneous noise) and then get so close to the mic that I am practically sticking it in my mouth when I talk. Good microphone technique is as important as, if not more important than, the quality of the mic you buy.

You are in the audio business, never forget that. I still hear BIG podcasts from major networks that sound as if the guests or even the hosts themselves are using AirPods or some other kind of phone headset. We can tell.

Wherever You Get Your Podcasts...

During a keynote I once delivered at a podcast conference, I talked about how newer podcast listeners are discovering shows on all kinds of platforms—platforms your podcast might not even be on (yet). I punctuated this by asking if when you end your show with "check us out wherever you get your podcasts," you are 100 percent sure about that.

Whenever we hit Publish, we have a publisher's-eye view of these platforms. We are like the mail carrier in our building here in Boston—toiling in a tiny room, putting that same direct-mail postcard into five hundred identical little boxes. But no two boxes are the same. In fact, every box is its own unique neighborhood.

And so, what *should* we say at the end of a show, if not "wherever you get your podcasts"? I have three answers to this, in increasing order of effectiveness:

1   Send them to your website. Every podcast should have its own domain and website where listening is enabled through the browser or through as many platforms as you care to list. The point is, if someone is directed to your website, they will be able to listen to the show somehow.

2   "Wherever you get your podcasts," but *really*. This means having a presence of some kind on every platform your ideal listener might inhabit, so that you can, in fact, keep your promise. And yes, that might mean YouTube.

3   Here's the real answer: if someone is listening to your podcast, you *know* where they "got your podcast." If

they are listening on an RSS-driven podcatcher, then they can follow you on that podcatcher. If they are listening to you on YouTube, then they can "MASH SUB-SCRIBE BELOW." If they are listening to you on Spotify, you can tell them exactly how to follow you there too. All of this is possible by preparing a slightly different version of your show for each platform. Isn't this one of the real promises of dynamic ad insertion technology? It isn't just for mattresses.

Full disclosure: I am a MASSIVE HYPOCRITE about Answer 3. I just barely get an audio file with a static image uploaded to YouTube each week in the meager time I have to record my daily podcast. It would probably add another hour or so to my workload each week, and I rarely have that. *I am the worst.* But if I were a full-time podcaster, you can bet I'd have custom versions of the show for every platform it is on.

Really, that's the true message here. Want to get really good at podcasting? Quit your job. You'll figure it out right quick.

Some have evolved their call to action over the years to be "Check us out/subscribe to us wherever you get your podcasts," which reads to me like a cry for help. Because if "wherever you get your podcasts" for a potential new listener is Instagram, YouTube, or SoundCloud, is your podcast even there?

In short, the podcasting space is becoming... messy. And it's not going to get neater as more and more podcast content ends up in decidedly non-podcast places. Which brings me to this existential question: What even *is* a podcast?

What Even *Is* a Podcast?

I have thought about this—a lot. There are a couple of ways this question can be parsed.

First, there is the strict, traditionalist view: a podcast can only be delivered as an enclosure using RSS in an open system. And I'm sympathetic to that definition. But it is a producer-based definition. Hitching your wagon to it is fraught with peril because it's format-based. Here are some other formats: 8-track, MiniDisc, VHS, Beta, Blu-ray. You see where I am going with this. Formats die. RSS will too, I can confidently say. It's already fading from view.

The other extreme is this definition: a podcast is any on-demand content that calls itself a podcast. I'm not sure I buy that one either. We have to draw a line somewhere. It's what separates us from the animals.

So here is where I have settled, in two parts:

1   If you can access it on a podcast client, it's a podcast.
2   The podcast is a subset of *The Show*.

I think the job of the podcast producer, first and foremost, is to put on a *show*. The podcast may be the primary manifestation of that, yes, but in order to not get drowned out and to maximize your chances of getting heard in this very confusing new era of podcasting, I think we need to consider "the podcast" as just one subset of what your real job is: to produce a *show*, and then put that show anywhere and everywhere it can be encountered.

So I want to leave you with a simple three-part model to increase your chances of success and getting heard in this crazy new era of big, fuzzy podcasting.

1   The first is just table stakes: BE *where they are.* And that means doing the work to put your content anywhere and everywhere it can be encountered *by your ideal listener.* I'll give you an example: I am in several Facebook groups for podcasters, and I see that channels like SoundCloud get panned by hosts and producers for various technical and support reasons. Maybe those things are true. But research shows that a high single-digit percentage of listeners have consumed a podcast there. Your not being there could frustrate a significant portion of your audience, if your target listener is a regular SoundCloud user (a great question for your survey… hint… hint…).

So, regardless of the fences that *you*, the producers, try to build, there's an audience, those rampaging feral hogs, on SoundCloud, digging up the turnips, out of your control. And you can substitute for "SoundCloud" any number of similar services that are not producer friendly. You don't matter in that equation.

2   The second part: LIVE *where they are.* This one requires a bit more work, but not much. Let's say you take my advice, consider what people should *see* when they listen to your podcast, and upload it to YouTube. Should the call to action at the end of that podcast be "Check us out wherever you get your podcasts"? Or "Subscribe to us on iTunes"? No—it should be to click the Subscribe button below the video. And on Spotify, it should be to follow you. And on SoundCloud, it should be to interact with you by commenting on the track. It should be native to the environment; remember, the

podcast is just a subset of the show. The podcast is the podcast. But the YouTube version of the podcast should be different enough to at least acknowledge it's on YouTube. We get lazy with submissions—but it's a small editing tweak to make your content *live* (as in, rhymes with "give"), natively, where you have uploaded the show.

3   Finally, *LOVE where they are*. Getting people to try your podcast *and* switch to a platform you'd rather they listen on is trying to change two behaviors at once, and the consumer behavior term for that is *no bueno*.

What that means to you is that all these channels we're talking about are not spokes that drive to a hub. The audience isn't going to be herded anywhere. So if you are putting your content on YouTube, you need to be a YouTuber. You need to get people to subscribe *there* and have a plan to extract the value of that audience *there*. A YouTube video may not be a podcast. But it is every bit as much a part of the show as your podcast.

The audience is out there. You won't attract them. You won't pull them to your site or to subscribe to you on your favorite podcast client. You have to put success in your way, *be* where they are, *live* where they are, and have a plan to *love* where they are.

YouTube? Really?

I mentioned YouTube in the last section, and here is an inconvenient truth: when you ask people where they "ever" listen to podcasts, YouTube comes up as the number one answer in survey after survey. (I've personally seen this at least ten times in various studies I have worked on.)

Hosting providers don't measure it. It doesn't show up in download trackers. And even some in the podcast industry deny it because, well, they don't want it to be true. But if you have shows on YouTube, you do count their metrics—you just count them as "views" or "impressions." But if a listener consumes their favorite podcast on YouTube, they are counting it as a "podcast," regardless of the fact that it isn't in the right silo. The listener is never wrong.

Still, YouTube ranks higher as a platform "ever used" than it does as the platform "most often used." This is the quirk of data that interests me. Often, but not always, when you ask a sample a series of questions about things you "ever" do and things you do "most often," the numbers may change, but the rank order of things generally doesn't. I won't say it never or rarely changes, but it usually doesn't. So, let's theorize about why that is.

First, Spotify and Apple are the two most popular podcast-listening platforms, and that makes a lot of sense. Both are built as listening-first platforms. You don't question these rankings. YouTube, however, shows up much stronger as something people "ever use." It's not the one they use the most—it's not necessarily built as a podcast app—but it gets used a lot. What else would it get used for? Why would so many people who otherwise use Spotify or Apple or Pocket Casts or Overcast or any other made-to-measure podcast app ever use YouTube?

I bet you already know the answer to this. It's the "easy button" for *finding* a quick piece of content right now to satiate your immediate entertainment needs. You are going to find something that captivates you right away. It might even recommend the next thing that captivates you. You might be there for *four hours* before you know it. It's built for that. It's built for discovery. It's built to grab you in the moment and keep you there with one video after another. It's not purpose-built to subscribe to a podcast. But it is built for you to *find* one.

What I would suggest is that maybe it makes sense just to dump your podcast on YouTube, and maybe it doesn't. (It probably doesn't.) It would be better if there were a video element—it definitely helps. I've conducted research showing that even a video of people talking into micro-phones helps with comprehension and engagement; the visual of the speaker gives the consumer something to focus on and a way to tell the players apart.

The fact that most people listen to audio-only podcasts doesn't mean they don't consume them on video plat-forms. It happens a lot. But think about the things you are interested in—maybe the things your podcast is about. Now imagine watching two videos in a row on YouTube that are about that thing you are passionate about. What aspects or elements of your show would naturally slot in between those two things? Make *that* thing.

Link that thing to your full podcast for people who want more or want something audio-forward for when they are in that mood. That thing might not be your podcast. It probably shouldn't be. But what that thing is, tailored to the medium of YouTube, is limited only by your imagination. What that thing could be is the best free ad for your podcast you could create. Maybe it's a clip or segment of your existing show, the interesting answer from a guest that doesn't need the question included, a funny joke, or something else immediately intriguing. Whatever it is, it should stand alone as a thing unto itself that can help your podcast get discovered.

I'm passionate about audio, and I will continue to view podcasting as a premier audio medium. But anytime I hear people grouse about podcasting's "discovery problem," I think about this.

SPEAKING OF DISCOVERY, it's about time people discovered your spanking new, retooled podcast. There is a *lot* of marketing advice for podcasters online, and much of it is good (as long as you keep the avatar of your ideal listener firmly in mind), so I am not going to retread a lot of tactical stuff, like posting on social media, that changes with the wind. Still, as you put up your Grand Opening sign, there are a few different ways to think about your podcast from the listener's perspective that I'd like you to consider. So let's hang up that sign and tackle a few of them in the next episode.

Episode Nine
The Grand Opening Sign

The "Findability" Problem

I was in a discussion recently about podcasting's "findability" problem. We do seem to spend a good deal of time talking about "findability" and discovery in podcasting, but I always find these topics somewhat distressing.

First, there's a lack of agency in this line of thinking. If you made a new breakfast cereal and it didn't sell, you wouldn't complain about the "supermarket discovery problem." You'd market your product better. Or maybe your cereal is bad.

I think podcasting has a findability problem in the same way that Delaware has a findability problem: if I had to, I could point to it on a map, but no one's given me a reason to go there. Podcasting has a *quality* problem. There is no better evidence of this than looking at the most up-to-date figures for the percentage of the population that has ever listened to a podcast, and the percentage that listens to at least one weekly. According to the most recent Infinite Dial study from Edison Research (2023), the percentage of Americans who have ever listened to a podcast is 64. The percentage who say they listen every week is 31. Less than a third.

There's your problem. If I gave the same two numbers for, say, pizza, they'd be 90 and 80.

So, why the big gaps between trial and usage? Why haven't more people made podcasting a regular habit? Why has a third of the country tried a podcast at least once but didn't listen to one in the last week?

I have never thought that the entire medium has a findability problem. I do think it has a perception problem, and any individual podcast has its own marketing challenges, but people are pretty good at finding things they want to find. Make better content. Make content that people *love*. They will recommend your podcast to like-minded friends and family. If you don't have a show that people would recommend like that, you are wasting your money buying advertising and paid promotion.

That's something I learned many years ago from doing soft launches and format changes in the radio business: never put up your Grand Opening sign if the shelves are dirty.

The Offline World

If there is one aspect of marketing and promotion that is criminally underused by podcasters, it's this: the offline world. Yes, there is a whole world out there, inhabited by real people visiting non-virtual places, and it doesn't disappear when you turn off your laptop.

I spent many years conducting advertising and marketing effectiveness studies for brands and advertisers so they could see what aspects of their ads were working and which ones weren't. Over all that time, the two most effective forms of advertising I encountered were podcasting (duh) and a general category of marketing we call "out-of-home," which means exactly what it sounds like.

Out-of-home (OOH) advertising is a broad category that encompasses everything from billboards to mall kiosks to gas pump ads to video screens in taxis. But for the most part, they all have something in common: a small, unique window that is contextually fixed, where the exclusive attention of a consumer can be earned for a short period of time.

Think about this—when we browse the web, we are bombarded with a withering torrent of advertising messages, from banners and skyscrapers to pop-ups and flyovers. A media site might blast a dozen different advertising messages at you before you even scroll down. It's exhausting! And all the eye-tracking software in the world can't tell you if any of it actually means anything in the brain of the viewer.

But now think about the last time you went to the movies. I bet, before the previews and the dancing candy boxes, you saw some ads for local and/or national businesses. You were the very definition of a captive audience: the theater is dark, and you are getting one very bright image instead of twenty display ads. The same thing happens when you take a taxi in New York City—the cab is equipped with a video screen that alternates clips from TV shows with ads. I bet you watched it.

The great thing about OOH advertising is that if you think it through, you can reach the exact ideal listener you are hoping to get to in a far more efficient way than blasting Facebook ads or social posts. Imagine you have a sports podcast (let's say it's better than *Two Superfans Talking about the Cubs* from earlier). It might be free to post social messages about it, and even cheap to buy some Facebook ads, but once you actually sit down and figure out the conversion percentages for these efforts, I bet you will be underwhelmed.

Imagine, instead, buying some posters in the restrooms of sports bars, right over the urinals. Heck, even buying custom urinal cakes, so guys can read about your podcast while they freshen and deodorize the space. The percentage of qualified leads in this scenario likely borders on 100 percent.

The great thing about this kind of advertising is that you don't have to eat the elephant all at once. If your brain flashed to what it would cost to buy run-of-toilet ads for Buffalo Wild Wings nationwide, this is not a thing you have to do. Start local—again, if your show is ready for the Grand Opening sign, you just need to start somewhere. If twenty-five people try your show after a weekend of sports bar advertising, and those new listeners tell their buddies, you are on your way. In fact, local advertising, period, is underused in podcasting. I certainly don't care where my listeners live. If I double my downloads even though my new listeners are all from my home city of Boston, this will trouble me not.

Events in general are a pretty good bet. Most cities and towns of a certain size have some kind of food-related festival, for instance. What a great place to set up a booth promoting your cooking podcast or cheese-making show! Again, the ratio of potentially interested people to not-interested people is vastly better than it would be from buying online ads, even if you could target that precisely with programmatic advertising.

I think podcasters often default to things like social promotion because it seems easy and/or cheap. But if you have done the work to really profile an ideal listener, all you have to do is think through where you can find those humans in real life. I guarantee putting in some effort in meatspace will vastly outperform the metaverse, every time.

And while we are on the topic of events . . .

Events

Podcast events are a lot of fun, and a great opportunity to turn what normally happens between the earbuds into a *genuinely* shared experience. A couple of years ago, I went to a live performance by the cast of *The White Vault* here in Boston, and it was wonderful to put faces to their (very talented) voices. But for shows like *Welcome to Night Vale*, or *Crime Junkie*, or even *Wait Wait . . . Don't Tell Me!*, events are also a big part of their revenue stream, and that stream is finally picking up again after COVID drove a screwdriver into the works.

I think this is a wonderful time to consider how any podcast can reach its audience in new and compelling ways with events—and these don't have to be big, expensive, theater-renting events. Any kind of festival or free event in your town is a great place to put up a table and a sign and put on a show. People will come by out of curiosity. If you can stock the audience with friends, you can even drum up a little social proof that might intrigue the passersby into stopping and listening and maybe taking a card or sticker.

Let's face it—we are lousy with "virtual events." And I don't know about you, but I am hardly watching any of them. My life is still Microsoft Teams and Zoom right now, and the thought of taking a break from Teams and Zoom to watch more Teams and Zoom sits somewhere between cleaning my bathroom and giving myself another quarantine haircut on my list of "leisure" activities. There is too much focus on the "virtual" and not enough on the "event." We miss Events with a capital *E*. And I think every podcast is capable of creating one.

Here are a few random thoughts about how you could put on a show for your show.

1 Make it special

For some podcasts, just doing your regular show before a live audience is enough of an "event" to be an Event, because your audience gets to have a level of access they typically never have. But now, I don't think that is enough to really stand out in an environment where the only variety in our days is what virtual background we are using. Pull out all the stops. Bring back guests from your best episodes. Pull in the biggest star you can grab. Redo some of your best bits.

The point is, don't treat it simply like a video version of your typical show. Treat it as though it's the last show you will ever do.

2 Make it scarce

Don't do this every week or even every quarter, or it's meaningless. A touring show like *Wait Wait... Don't Tell Me!* could do the same podcast in one city after another without alteration, thanks to the magic of geography. With your podcast and a limited budget, that's not going to fly. I have a lot of friends who are keynote speakers, and they are grappling with the same thing: If you basically give the same speech from city to city, but cities and events have been replaced by Zoom, can you really keep giving your same speech?

There are really two ways to go about this: time separation between events or limiting the audience. One of the most delightful activities I discovered during COVID lockdowns was the online "dinner parties" being held by the cooking empire of Barbara Lynch, one of Boston's most successful restaurateurs. You signed up for a two-hour class with one of her chefs, picked up all the ingredients at the takeout window of one of her restaurants, and then cooked with just a *handful* of other online students to make the dinner in real time. It was being able to see all the other participants, and not just feeling like you were watching TV, that made it engaging.

Now, you don't have to limit class size online, but they did; and it made the event special precisely because it was scarce—only a handful of people could take part. This meant my Zoom screen wasn't an existential *Brady Bunch* nightmare, *and* the teaching staff was constantly calling me by name and asking to see how I was doing.

I made prune-stuffed homemade gnocchi with foie gras sauce. I am sorry, dear readers, but I am already very happily married.

3 Turn the chairs around

My good friend Chris Brogan likes to say that the difference between an audience and a community is which direction the chairs are facing. With Barbara Lynch's online "dinner parties," the chairs had been turned to face each other, and the experience was richer for it. Your podcast (like all podcasts) is largely a one-to-many affair, but a virtual live event is a great opportunity for you to rethink that relationship entirely, break the "fourth wall," and invite your audience in to co-create the experience.

Letting in those listeners who want to be a part of the show whenever possible is always good advice, whether for an event or the regular show. Even people who would never call the request line at a radio station like to know that it's at least possible. Acknowledging your audience as integral to the show and its content is something you really can't do enough of. Some people will take you up on it, some won't. But it will mean something to almost all of them.

Keep Your Feed Warm

If you ask a hundred podcast experts to name the three best promotional strategies they have, ninety-five will say that cross-promotion with other podcasts is one of them. There is absolutely no doubt that being promoted by a like-minded podcast (and returning the favor) is one of the most efficient ways to reach likely listeners and tap into a kind of "network effect" for podcasting. Still, I think there is an even more powerful way to take advantage of these "near worlds" of other podcasts to make it even easier for our listeners.

Certainly, the bigger networks benefit from symbiotic cross-promotion. If you like one show from NPR or Wondery, chances are you are going to like a similar show from the same network. But what is understated about cross-promotion is the power of the brand umbrella that sits *over* "Podcast A" and "Podcast B." It's why *S-Town* did so well. It wasn't one podcast recommending another random podcast; it was a recommendation that fit under a strong brand (*This American Life*) that you already knew and trusted. This is the importance of *brand* in podcasting.

That's also why some people continue to think there are new episodes of the podcast *Serial* coming out every week, when the show has actually produced only three seasons since 2014—a span of ten years! This is because the *New York Times*, which owns *Serial*, dumped other podcasts into the Serial feed, like *Nice White Parents* and *The Improvement Association*. While those shows were not *Serial*, they showed up in your podcast player as if they were a sub-brand or "special edition" of *Serial*, if you were subscribed to that RSS feed. They probably couldn't get away with dropping a show about UFC fighting in there, but they took a good, calculated risk that people who liked *Serial* would like *Nice White Parents* and not unsubscribe. It works because of the brand promise of the Serial feed.

This is even more compelling than cross-promotion— it's essentially forced trial. Well, no one is *forced* to listen to a podcast (I think that is against the Geneva Convention), but you get my point. The new show can be delivered to likely listeners without their having to lift a finger, which is an enormous competitive advantage.

So, what is the indie podcaster to do to compete with this?

The key to building a brand in podcasting today is not your *show*. It's your *feed*: the RSS address people subscribe to to get your show automatically delivered with every new episode. It is going to be really hard for your show to stand out in a universe where so much listening goes to so few shows. There are literally millions of podcasts out there tied at 100 or fewer listeners. If you could increase that to 1,000, you would *immediately* be in another tier of listening, and things could start happening for you with recommendations and charts. This is difficult for a new indie show. But consider what you could do to get your *feed* up to 1,000 listeners. I bet you can do it in a *week* if you are diligent and know your space well.

When you are competing against one of the large networks for earballs, you aren't competing against a show—you are competing against a brand that stands for a thing, reliably delivers that thing across multiple shows, and delivers that thing weekly if not daily in some fashion or another. It's why *Up First* is such a big show—it delivers what you know, like, and trust about the NPR news brand reliably, consistently, and frequently. My podcast, on the other hand, might reliably sound like me, but it sure as heck isn't frequent or even consistent. Yes, I am admitting I will never beat NPR.

But a feed could be all those things. A feed could deliver like-minded content of consistent quality, reliably and frequently. I could not name all the individual NBA-related shows on *The Ringer*. I don't even know if *The Ringer* could. Seems like the names change. But it doesn't matter—I subscribe to *The Ringer* NBA feed, and I reliably get on-brand, hoops-related entertainment daily. It's there when I push the button every single day. I might not listen every day, but I know it's there when I want it.

Am I advocating for joining or creating a network? It needn't be so ambitious. There are thousands of marketing podcasts (I used to do one) of varying quality and not so many big ones. But aggregate them into a network, as my friend Jason Falls has done with his Marketing Podcast Network, and all of a sudden you've got a little reach. And reach begets reach.

Now, building a network can be just as daunting as it sounds. Instead, you could think about which other podcasts in your niche share a similar approach or ethos, and just build a single feed that stands for something and delivers on-topic content reliably and frequently, aggregating your podcast and some like-minded, on-topic alternatives, so that there is always something new in the feed even if your show isn't new.

This is the path to building habits. It's tough growing an audience when you put out one show every week or two, take breaks, or do "seasons." But a single feed that delivers the best thinking in marketing or sales or dentistry every day—your show on a Monday, someone else's on Tuesday, etc.—this is a thing you can build a brand around to grow the audiences for all the podcasts involved.

To put it another way—how are the leading podcast networks dominating the space right now? Consolidation. But consolidation isn't only an option for the "haves." If you can't beat 'em, you can join *someone*. Start there.

Think about it. It is going to be increasingly difficult to compete in the podcasting space over the next few years. The growth in the total hours spent listening to podcasts is going to slow—that's just nature. If someone makes time in their lunch hour every day for 15 minutes of content relevant to their job or life, being the feed that provides that every day is the surest path to building a habit and then a relationship. People don't fire their friends.

OSHIT

Finally, I think we need to acknowledge something that I am sure you are painfully aware of by now—it is really hard to build an audience. Part of the challenge is that podcasting doesn't have very many "hits" in the same way as other media—those new HBO or Netflix shows that all your friends are talking about and you have to watch so you can keep up with the conversation.

In another life I used to do the music testing for what was then the largest pure play radio company. This involved hundreds of nights, all over the world, playing hundreds of thousands of eight-second snippets of songs: the "hook" of the song that provided the shortest distance from "I hear this" to "I know this and like this." In my life I've heard millions of hooks. This is not hyperbole—I am good at math. And I can give you two of the key ingredients for the success of these hooks: *melody* and *harmony*. Does a hit need both? Not necessarily. Does it need at least one? It is pretty hard to have a hit without it. It's not impossible—I mean, "Sabotage" by the Beasties has a terrible hook, but it's more of an outlier than the norm.

I don't think the current crop of pop songs is as melodic as, say, the Hot 100 from thirty years ago. I'm not making a value judgment here—you don't *need* melody—but there is less of it in today's hits, which (aside from Taylor Swift and a handful of other outliers) are performing worse than ever. Then you have harmony—the voices singing together to make the whole greater than the sum of its parts. Again, you don't need harmony. But without harmony we wouldn't have the Eagles. Or Bone Thugs-n-Harmony. Again, there are outliers, but without either melody or harmony, your would-be hit starts at a real disadvantage.

So let me present my Oversimplified Superstring Hit Incubation Theory (OSHIT). I think there is a construct of melody and harmony that applies to the hits in *any* medium—including podcasting. Melody is that thing that makes a new hit quickly singable. There might be a quadrillion songs on Spotify, but there aren't a quadrillion melodies. The melody is the familiar (or almost familiar) handle you can grab onto when you are presented with something new.

Don't know if you might like this new show about crime scene investigation in Miami? Did you like *csi*? You will at least start *csi: Miami* or *csi: Vegas* knowing the melody, if not the words. *Hobbs & Shaw* might not carry the *Fast and Furious* moniker, but again you will know the melody. Why was "Smells Like Teen Spirit" such a HUGE song when it could have been just another angsty grunge-fest or punk moshfest? Because it sounded like Boston's "More Than a Feeling." It was angry, but it was *familiar* first, even though it was new.

The melody of a hit is the hummable part, the instantly memorable throughline that is already familiar to you. In yet another life, I taught rhetoric to first-year students at the main campus of Penn State. In rhetoric, we refer to a thing called the "Known-New Contract." If you start an argument on familiar turf, you can introduce the "new" part of the argument on a firmer footing. It's the spoonful of sugar that helps the medicine go down, kinda like this whole book.

If the melody in my OSHIT construct is the familiar hook of a potential hit, the harmony is getting people to sing it all together. Velocity requires *synchronicity*—not just that we are all consuming a particular thing, but that we are doing it at the same time. Did you watch *Tiger King*?

Yes, you did. Did you watch *Tiger King* season two? No, you did not. At least I did not. Was *Tiger King* good? Eh. It was *bananas*, but on the grand scale of documentaries, it wasn't exactly *Shoah* or *The Thin Blue Line* or *March of the Penguins*. But we all watched it at the same time because we were all sent home from our jobs that week and we were cold and frightened and starved for connection and we needed to feel as though we were part of the same life as our friends and families and co-workers.

This is why the all-time ratings champs on TV are sporting events, live finales, and awards shows. These are forced synchronous events. It's also why releasing *Dune* simultaneously in theaters and on HBO Max killed its box office—there was no shared urgency.

Podcasting largely lacks harmony. When you can listen to a podcast anytime, there is little compunction to listen to one at *any* given time. They are always there—convenient, but rarely urgent. In other words, asynchronous. And they also currently (though not by definition) lack melody. The whole *medium* is new to so many people, and even for veteran listeners, there isn't exactly the equivalent of *NCIS: New Orleans* or *Thursday Night Football* or the Traveling Wilburys—that thread of familiarity that telegraphs immediately, if you like *this*, you will like *that*.

Even some of the biggest hits of podcasting aren't easy to explain to a friend. That's part of why there is such a spate of celebrity podcasts right now. What is easier to describe to people: "It's the Michelle Obama podcast," or "It's the podcast that reveals the stories behind the world's most recognizable and interesting sounds"? By the way, that second podcast (*Twenty Thousand Hertz*) is REALLY, REALLY GOOD and I RARELY MISS IT, but most times when I try to recommend it to others, I end up falling back on lengthy examples or "You just have to hear it." Look, I am not even trying one of those tiny Vienna sausage samples on a stick in the supermarket, let alone giving an hour to a completely unfamiliar concept of a podcast.

Again, there are outliers to everything, but I would submit that so little of the Top 50 podcast list looks like the Top 50 of anything else that maybe the whole medium is—currently—an outlier. And yes, that makes it a beautiful thing. But if you want to have a *hit*, sure, you can cross-promote, buy ads, even pay influencers, and maybe some of that will work. But beyond the tactics of the hit, there is the meta-structure of a hit: How can you create a podcast that has melody—a quickly familiar strain—and harmony—a thing we *need* to listen to, not whenever and wherever, but *tonight on the way home*? These are the tough questions creators need to think about.

To achieve harmony, it's best to think of your podcast, whether it is new or five years old, as if it is going to have a world premiere on a given date or for a specific upcoming episode. If you have a hundred pennies a year to spend on promoting your show, spend all of them in multiple channels over a very short period of time rather than spreading them out over the course of a year. And try promoting an *episode*, which seems like a lot less of a commitment than the show. If you think about the moments that really created some of the biggest podcasts in America, they were singular moments—Joe Rogan interviewing

Bernie Sanders or Elon Musk; Marc Maron interviewing Barack Obama.

One of the great things about unscripted podcasts is that you can really listen to them in any order, with the exception of daily news shows, which obsolete themselves daily. If you could get *one* special show in front of potential listeners and have them hear about it more than one way, this is how you create synchronicity and velocity. Asking someone to commit to listening to your show is a lot, especially with how time-starved we perceive ourselves to be. But maybe you have a better chance of selling people on one episode, and not just next week's episode. Make it *the* episode—the best thing you can make—and put your best foot forward. Ground it in the familiar, and then surprise and delight with your own unique twist.

Melody and harmony.

We've just about reached the end of our show here, but before we go, I want to revisit "melody" and how difficult it is to "pitch" our podcast to people.

Post-roll

So You Have a Show—
Now What?

_____

The Pitchable Podcast

I get pitched a lot of podcasts. A frightening number, really. I can't possibly listen to all of them, or even some of them—it is hard enough trying to keep up with my own clients. One dubious benefit of this, however, is that I have become one of the world's leading experts on terrible podcast pitches. I've got my 10,000 hours and everything.

It is hard to pitch a podcast—but I hope, after this book, it is a little easier. If you are having a hard time crafting a compelling pitch for your show, may I humbly suggest that's because you are having a hard time differentiating it and highlighting something unique and compelling that would get someone's attention in a sea of bad pitches. This is a pitch problem, and it is also a podcast problem.

The solution to this is to get laser-focused on a specific listener and surprise and delight that listener, which has been the focus of this entire book. When you have done the work outlined here, you will find the vocabulary to paint a much more compelling picture of your podcast by tapping into what it does, rather than what it's about.

Still, we are all going to be put in situations where we have to pitch our podcast in some kind of short, compelling way, whether that's to an advertiser or just to the person sitting next to you at dinner. It's more than just a communication—you are hoping to drive action. So I talked to the most knowledgeable expert I know about change communication—my wife, Tamsen Webster. Yes, I was so compelled by her work that I married the company.

Tamsen has crafted a number of methodologies for helping people get clarity on their big idea and communicate that idea in a way that catalyzes change. She typically does this for companies, start-ups, and founders, but you can read a wonderful guide to her way of thinking in her book *Find Your Red Thread* (also available from Page Two, which published this book). I asked her to apply her prodigious brain to the problem and come up with a framework for the Pitchable Podcast, which I am delighted to share with you here.

Tamsen has a framework for change communication that she calls the Conversational Case—as in, making a case for something. It's not a script you read to someone verbatim, but it gives you the clarity to talk succinctly and persuasively about your podcast when you are telling someone what you do. I'll walk you through the elements here and then show you how I would fill this out for my own podcast *Sounds Profitable*.

The Conversational Case
...For "The Pitchable Podcast"

The world isn't looking for a new podcast—and they certainly aren't looking for yours—yet! Telling prospective listeners, sponsors, and guests about your podcast means having to make the case for it. To do that, they have to hear the answers to the questions that their brain is looking for, not what you think they should hear. They have to hear a case that makes sense to them—and feels natural to you. Use this Pitchable Podcast framework to start, or summarize, your thinking about your podcast's Red Thread®.

"In my experience with..."

_____

type of category or audience

GOAL

"they often want to know..."

_____

common question your podcast addresses or illuminates

"so they can..."

_____

goal to achieve

PROBLEM

"When looking for that answer…"

☐ they
☐ the market

"often focus(es) on…"

_____

current perspective

☐ Rather
☐ More

"than on…"

_____

new perspective

TRUTH

"Yet we all…"

☐ believe
☐ can agree it's true

_____

key finding, value, belief, or discovery

CHANGE

"That's why my podcast addresses
the audience's needs by…"

_____

_____

_____

your unique approach

OPTIONAL: ACTION(S)

"Which not only answers their question
(and achieves their goal), it also…"

_____

_____

_____

additional key benefit(s) or "free prize"

"In each episode, we deliver on this promise with…"

_____

_____

_____

_____

anchors, benchmarks, and qualities of each episode

"So, would you..."

☐ be open(-minded) to
☐ consider

_____

_____

first action you want your audience to take

Now, I love this simple-looking worksheet, because it is not so simple. I held it back until the end of the book because I don't think you can adequately fill it out until you have gotten a lot more clarity on the essential question we worked on earlier: Who are you for? When you know who you are for, you have a much clearer sense of what your potential listeners are dealing with, what other options or sources they might have watched or listened to, and the whole consideration set that informs their information and entertainment choices.

Filling this worksheet out forces you to confront a number of words like "unique," "new," and "discovery." You are in a better position to answer this now, because you have spent some time listening to other podcasts in your topic, and you have pitched your show to be more valuable, useful, and delightful to your specific audience than those other podcasts.

I hope I don't have to say this, but where it says "type or category of audience," don't write "Women 25–54" or I shall become quite cross with you. Also, this really doesn't work with a fiction podcast, but again, that is a writer problem as much as a podcaster problem.

Now that you have the complete framework of this book behind you, maybe some new questions for conversations or survey research will present themselves to you: What else do I need to know to really fill this out with purpose? What are my knowledge gaps—about both my audience and my subject? These are all excellent questions. For a detailed guide on the process here, I highly encourage you to pick up a copy of *Find Your Red Thread*. I think you'll see why Tamsen and I get along so famously.

Here's how I filled out mine for the *Sounds Profitable* podcast, by the way.

"In my experience with…"

podcasters
_____

type of category or audience

GOAL

"they often want to know…"

how to master their craft and become better
_____

common question your podcast addresses or illuminates

"so they can…"

grow their audience and revenue
_____

goal to achieve

PROBLEM

"When looking for that answer…"

☑ they
☐ the market

"often focus(es) on…"

how to market their show

current perspective

☑ Rather
☐ More

"than on…"

making their show more marketable

new perspective

TRUTH

"Yet we all…"

☐ believe
☑ can agree it's true

the audience controls your destiny

key finding, value, belief, or discovery

CHANGE

"That's why my podcast addresses
the audience's needs by..."

giving them data-driven insights to understand

their audience and industry

your unique approach

OPTIONAL: ACTION(S)

"Which not only answers their question
(and achieves their goal), it also..."

gives them the tools to create endless amounts

of relevant content

additional key benefit(s) or "free prize"

"In each episode, we deliver on this promise with..."

wit, wisdom, and exclusive industry data from the leading

audience researcher in audio, and his experience working

with the most successful audio companies in the world

anchors, benchmarks, and qualities of each episode

"So, would you..."

☐ be open(-minded) to
☐ consider

_____

first action you want your audience to take

I left off the optional action step, but you get the picture. And yes, you can listen to my podcast at sounds profitable.com/podcast/.

Twenty Last Thoughts

We have reached the end, my friends. By now, I hope you have gained some clarity on the following:

- Shifting from the podcast you want to make to the podcast they want to hear.

- The importance of knowing who you are for and who you are not for.

- The value of research to spark creativity and provide useful constraints.

- The answer to why someone would, or would not, listen to your podcast.

- How to talk to listeners about your show, and how to field your own survey.

- How to create a vivid, detailed listener profile.

- Building a show that makes sense to your ideal listener with no wasted effort.

- Providing a safe space for your audience.

- A different way to think about editing.

- The power of the offline world for reaching listeners.

- … And, of course, the OSHIT theory.

This is a lot of work. I hope you keep this book close by for as long as you are creating podcasts. I have taken great pains to write a book that won't go out of date; I firmly believe this book will be useful, without any additions or edits, fifty years from now. These are the basics of crafting an entertainment and reaching a listener, and those fundamentals don't go out of style.

I leave you now with the Tom Webster Top 20. Thank you for reading and sharing this time with me.

1   No one has the right to an audience. No one deserves an audience. An audience has to be earned, every single show.

2   Millions of people still do not even know what a podcast is, or they have a mistaken impression that podcasts don't give them anything they don't already have. Prove them wrong every show.

3   There's no worse feeling than releasing a show that doesn't meet your own standards or level of ability. So don't do it. Put it under the bed. Quality trumps consistency. There are a lot of terrible, consistent podcasts.

4   Most people today are not fans of podcasting; they are fans of a show. Don't assume they come back to podcasting when they finish with the show.

5   If you tell your audience to listen to your show wherever they get their podcasts, be sure you know the answer to that one. You might not like it.

6   I hate to tell you this, but you need a visual strategy if you want to be discovered.

7 Don't spend money advertising your show if there is money to be spent making your show better. Nothing is worse than a grand opening if the shelves are dirty.

8 Promo swaps and feed swaps are great—but don't assume a true crime listener wants another true crime podcast. Find a show with a similar audience, not necessarily the same topic.

9 Your mic doesn't matter. Your interface doesn't matter. Your workstation doesn't matter. But for most people, sound quality *does* matter. Except for the hardcore fan, no one will sit through bad audio.

10 Podcast ads are not the devil. There is no evidence that people will leave your show if you run ads—even bad ones. If people leave your show because of an ad, you never had them to begin with.

11 For someone to add your show to their media diet, something else has to go. What is that? Can you message around that?

12 Similarly, the key to a habit is communicating the context in which people might listen to your show. Otherwise, they will just fit it in "whenever," which translates to "not often."

13 Use audience feedback, but carefully. Find ways to add value in exchange for feedback. And if your show is shrinking, the people still listening have less to tell you than you think.

14 The most underutilized way to market podcasts is in the offline world. Where are your listeners when they are receptive to your show? Urinal cake advertising in sports bars is better than X/Twitter for a sports show.

15 Your content should challenge, entertain, or come from genuine expertise. Hopefully two of those three, but I'll settle for one.

16 Two dudes rapping about the Cubs is not a podcast. It's a cry for help. Build a *show*. Your competition isn't another Cubs podcast. It's TikTok.

17 Your audience is a direct reflection of your show. Mean-spirited emails? Snarky voice feedback? Haters? Think about how you attracted them.

18 Everyone on your show needs a job. No wasted words.

19 There is no more important question to answer than why someone does, or does not, listen to your show.

20 I lied. Equally important is the answer to this question: Who are you for?

I wish you great success. The audience is listening.

Acknowledgments

THIS BOOK IS THE PRODUCT of thirty years in the business of audio; as such, hundreds of people shaped how I think about building shows and making audience-focused content. I could never thank them all. Still, there are a few people whose influence on my career and my passion for great audio could never be overstated.

I probably wouldn't even be in this business without Frank Cody and Brian Stone, who gave me my first start in media research back in the '90s with Broadcast Architecture. The unbelievable experiences I had there, working for some of the absolute biggest radio stations in the world as a young twentysomething kid, are simply not replicable today. More than that, though, Frank and Brian continued to be my models in life for how to treat employees, partners, and people in general long after I left their employ. Not a day goes by that I don't think of something they taught me about kindness, integrity, and doing the right thing.

As a young consultant in the radio business, I got to work with some amazingly talented programmers and executives who taught me very clearly about the art and science of audience research and turning that data into *entertainment*. Without them, I would have never graduated from analysis to instinct. I truly learned from the best, and the best learned from Steve Rivers and Guy Zapoleon. I was very, very fortunate to have had the honor of working with those two extensively, early in my career—nobody knew what made a *hit* better than they did.

I spent eighteen years of my career with Edison Research. It was there that I really honed my abilities as a data storyteller, thanks to the trust of Larry Rosin, Joe Lenski, and Rob Farbman, who set the standard for doing things right when it comes to audience research. And nothing I did there would have been possible without Mel Kiesche, Nicole Beniamini, Megan Lazovick, Melissa DeCesare, Eric Riddles, Sean Ross, Laura Silvia, Laura Ivey, Gabriel Soto, and Salma Aly. You were and are a magnificent team.

Certainly, the most consequential chapter in my life was my brief run as a start-up founder in London, building Puremix with Keith Pringle and Ande Macpherson. They remain dear, dear friends and were so patient with me as I came up with fifty ways to reinvent wheels in nonround ways. What we learned together there about the relationship between music taste, personality, and lifestyle behaviors remains some of the best work I've ever been part of, and it showed in the product we built. I still get weepy thinking about it. Keith and Ande are ferociously talented people and have forgotten more about developing audiences than I'll ever know.

A special thanks to Bryan Barletta, my partner at Sounds Profitable, who enabled my Great Leap from media researcher to finally devote my career to podcasting full-time. He is the best executor I've ever met—his superpower truly is momentum—and he has turned my whack-a-doodle ideas into actual reality. I am forever grateful for his openness, his ability to move people to action, and, most importantly, for his being a good human and friend.

None of this happens without my constant beam, Tamsen Webster. Three keys to a successful relationship are kindness, communication, and intimacy—but there is a fourth that doesn't get talked about: when you love someone, you champion them like a lion. She has always been my champion, and I will always be hers. I adore you, Tamsen.

About the Author

TOM WEBSTER is partner at Sounds Profitable, dedicated to setting the course for the future of audio. He has thirty years of experience in streaming, podcasting, audiobooks, terrestrial radio, and everything else that we stick in our earballs. In his previous work, with Edison Research, Webster was the co-author of the annual Infinite Dial® study, the longest-running study of consumer media habits since 1998, as well as the Share of Ear® and Edison Podcast Metrics studies. With Sounds Profitable, his body of work includes dozens of the most influential reports in podcasting, and he is one of the most widely cited audio researchers in the world.

Tom is an expert on audience behavior and has worked for some of the largest media properties, shows, and podcasts in the world. He has conducted research for syndicated programs such as *The Howard Stern Show* and *Elvis Duran and the Morning Show*, consulted the radio station with the largest weekly reach in the world, and currently works with over half of the Top 50 podcasts and Top 20 podcast networks. He once designed and executed the largest study of consumer music tastes in UK history, and he has provided audience and research consultation services on six continents.

Tom has performed card magic for Paula Abdul, shared a martini with Tom Jones, and can recommend your next new favorite album.

Made in the USA
Columbia, SC
12 September 2024

41872919R00129